GETTING TO THE FOOT
OF THE MOUNTAIN

T0315852

Lisa Evans

GETTING TO THE FOOT
OF THE MOUNTAIN

OBERON BOOKS
LONDON

First published in 2002 by Oberon Books Ltd
521 Caledonian Road, London N7 9RH
Tel: +44 (0) 20 7607 3637 / Fax: +44 (0) 20 7607 3629
e-mail: info@oberonbooks.com
www.oberonbooks.com

A catalogue record for this book is available from the British Library.

PB ISBN: 9781840023046
E ISBN: 9781786822000

Cover design by lpp

eBook conversion by Lapiz Digital Services, India.

To Gwenda

Thank you

Characters

DANIELLE
twenty-eight

KATH
her mother

PHYLLY
Kath's adopted sister

MO
their friend

DAVE
Mo's husband

BRIAN
Phylly's husband

CRAIG MCGELLAN

DEREK
Danielle's father

FELIX
Kath's boyfriend

Brian and Derek should be played by the same actor

Dave and Felix should be played by the same actor

The action takes place over one night in 2002

ACT ONE

*It is night. The sound of doors slamming shut. DANIELLE
– a photographer – is in her flat, until yesterday shared with
her latest boyfriend. She is packing up her stuff. A cardboard
box is spilling out of the understairs cupboard to one side. She
pulls out an old battered football, playing with it as she talks.*

DANIELLE: Rain on the window. Reflection of a woman, me
Danielle – in transit. Wanting to move forward. But from
where, to where? And why now? Sometimes you don't see
the endings coming, do you? The final shot is a surprise.
Cut to credits before you've finished gasping out, 'Wait a
minute, I'm not ready for this!' And I'm not. Sitting up all
night, dividing up blame along with the books and glasses
and photos. A collector of images.
A soul catcher. That's what he called me. Disastrous rela-
tionship number…well, who's counting? I don't.
I observe. From a distance. My job. Soul catcher! That'd
raise a few laughs at the paper. I don't want to be here.
I don't want to be stuck in the reeds thinking it's all over.
I want to be the camera, pulling back, to see the lake and
know the rain will come and float me off and away. That's
what I want. Perspective. And rain. We all know one step
leads to another, but it's hard to recall their order. (*She
looks at the ball and puts it by one of the packing cases, goes to
the stairs.*) Sometimes it seems as if I spent the whole of
my childhood sitting on the stairs, watching them through
the half open door – Phylly, my mum and Mo. My feet
turning numb in the draft from the gap in the front door
where someone had once, so the story goes, tried to kick in
the panel. Probably one of the McGellan boys. They were
responsible for every bit of vandalism, theft and wrongdo-
ing over a fifteen mile radius, according to my mother. I
thought they were magnificent. I was praying I'd get to sit
next to Craig, the sixth and youngest McGellan when we
both started school the next day.

Scene 1

Winter 1978. Chronological order: Three.

Kitchen, night. Three women in their 30's at a kitchen table, covered with the remains of supper. The room is barely furnished for economic rather than design reasons. PHYLLY opens another bottle of red wine. DANIELLE watches from the stairs.

KATH: We're going to regret this in the morning.

PHYLLY: Why?

MO: We always do. (*Shouting up at the ceiling.*) Boys, go to sleep! Little buggers.

PHYLLY: Where is Derek tonight?

DANIELLE: I knew the answer to that. I remember my father mainly as a series of bags in the hall. That night he'd picked up a kit bag, that meant badminton.

KATH: Squash. No. Badminton.

MO: He seems very keen.

KATH: I hope they don't keep Danielle awake.

PHYLLY: They always do.

KATH: Yes but it's her first day tomorrow. Reception 8:45 on the dot. I bet Derek forgets.

MO: You don't both have to take her do you?

KATH: (*Proudly.*) Dada took me.

PHYLLY: I'll come with you if you like. Before I go.

KATH: I don't think an aunt is quite the same.

PHYLLY: (*Sarcastic.*) Really?

KATH: Anyway. Go where?

PHYLLY: You being mean with the gas again Kath? It's colder than charity in here.

KATH: Where are you going?

MO: I think the snow's settling.

KATH: Phylly?

PHYLLY: We'll be all right in the van.

KATH: For Christ's sake where are you going?

PHYLLY: London.

MO: She's going to London. Weather permitting.

KATH: What for?

PHYLLY: Kicks? Life? Time to move on.

KATH: But you can't.

PHYLLY: Who says? I've exhausted all my options here.

KATH: What about Mum and Dada?

PHYLLY: They're not that decrepit.

KATH: You know Mum can't cope.

PHYLLY: Oh come on. She's not been in a bin for two years now. Besides she's got you.

KATH: After all they've done for you.

PHYLLY: Their choice.

KATH: Oh shut up. You knew and you didn't tell me?

PHYLLY: I wonder why.

KATH: What van?

(*Silence.*)

What van? You're not! You are not leaving here in Dan McGellan's van!

PHYLLY: What do you suggest, the fucking roof rack? Jesus, Kath, the man's kindly giving me a lift, not a leg over.

DANIELLE: I found evesdropping, particularly when my Aunt Phylly was a member of the trio, had widened my vocabulary to a point where the playground held no fears for me. Mum and Phylly were arguing so loud they didn't hear the hammering on the front door. It was accompanied by a whimpering drizzling sound as if there was a wounded creature out there in the snow-filled dark. Craig McGellan? (*CRAIG stands there, also five years old, grubby, poor and in shock.*)

It was a dream come true. Except for the tears making track marks down his dirty face. What do you want? (*MO approaches DANIELLE.*)

MO: Who is it? Danielle?

CRAIG: My dad was pushing the van. He won't get up. He's in the snow. He's all cold.

KATH: What's going on?

MO: His dad's hurt. Where is he?

CRAIG: Under the van.

PHYLLY: Oh shit.

MO: Phylly call an ambulance. Come on Kath. (*To CRAIG.*) Show us where he is.

KATH: (*To DANIELLE, who is preparing to follow them.*) You.

Stay here.

(*CRAIG, MO and KATH exit. Lights down on the house as DANIELLE follows them out. Behind her DEREK in a tracksuit enters and puts down his kit bag in the hall by the stairs.*)

DANIELLE: I didn't, of course. I followed them and saw, through the flurries of snow like the shaker my Grandad had given me for Christmas, my first dead body. As they loaded the grey faced Mr McGellan into the ambulance his arm flopped down. Just like he was waving. Craig had gone by then, taken away by Mum and Mo, so I waved back for him. Didn't seem much to stay for after that. So I went home.

(*DANIELLE turns back to the house and sees, silhouetted, the figures of DEREK/a man and PHYLLY embracing.*)

Between silhouettes and shadows I wondered who Aunt Phylly was kissing this time. I was suddenly too cold to care. Quietly, so's not to interrupt anything, I climbed carefully over the kit bag in the hall and shivered my way up the stairs to bed.

(*DANIELLE takes out a sports bag from the understairs cupboard.*)

I like covering the sports events. When I get the chance. He who has gone, or was driven away – anyway He plays football on the weekends. He told me he was called Striker. So that's what went in the paper. I didn't know it was a nickname. He rang up to complain. The rest as they say was history. Mostly I get fêtes and weddings. Not a lot of funerals though. For them you just collect old snapshots to go with the obit. When I was fourteen my grandad gave me a Kodak instamatic. I took a picture of him. Then he died. I don't think the two events were connected.

Scene 2

Spring 1988. Chronological order: Nine.

DANIELLE sits at the side of the kitchen desultorily arranging sandwiches on a plate as MO and KATH enter.

KATH: I can't believe it. Today of all days she has to upstage everyone.

MO: She does look…spectacular doesn't she. Oh hello Danielle, shouldn't you be lying down?

DANIELLE: I'm all right.

MO: Kath. Do you want all these put out now or save some for later?

KATH: Call me old fashioned but it really strikes me as out of order that her entrance created more of a stir than that of the coffin.

(*MO waves the plate of food at her.*)

Oh put them all out. Sooner they eat sooner they go.

(*DAVE enters full of bounce.*)

DAVE: Okey dokey, what can I do to help? How're you bearing up Kath? All right? Your mum's gone back to her room.

KATH: Her room?

DAVE: Well that's what she said. Phylly's taking care of her.

KATH: Good of her. For how long?

DAVE: She didn't say. Your sister's certainly done well for herself down London. PA she said. Bet you're pleased to have her back. Nothing like family in times like these.

MO: Dave. Why don't you take these through?

DAVE: They're going through your spread like locusts. If it wasn't such a sad event it'd be a great party. Shame your dad had to miss it.

(*KATH turns away.*)

MO: Dave!

DAVE: Sorry old thing. I didn't mean…

MO: No, you never do. Go and make sure our Steven's not getting drunk.

DAVE: Okey dokey. Give us a hug first.

MO: You've got *vol au vent* all down your tie.

DAVE: I was saving that for later. (*Exits.*)

MO: You all right?

KATH: How could she? Nothing but a handful of postcards in ten years and then she just wafts in and takes over!

MO: He was her dad too I suppose. Tell me something, has Dave always been like this?

KATH: Like what?

MO: I don't know. Phylly would know the word. Sort of… doggy.

KATH: I'm not really sure. But if I catch him humping the loose covers he'll be down the vets before he can say Bonio.

(*They both laugh. KATH's goes on too long then turns into tears. MO hugs her.*)

MO: That's it. You let it go. Danielle throw us some kitchen roll.

KATH: I can't get it into my head. He's always been there, my whole life.

DANIELLE: And mine. But as usual, no one was listening.

KATH: I don't know what we'd have done without Dada after Derek…you know.

(*DANIELLE goes back to her corner and sits.*)

MO: Left you.

KATH: Dada was always there for me. He made me feel safe. From when I was two and cut my knee falling off my tricycle to last month when those vandals graffitied the front wall.

DANIELLE: No prizes for guessing who she thought those vandals were.

KATH: Those McGellans should be locked up. Terrorists in the making, he called them, the entire family.

DANIELLE: It wasn't Craig's tag.

KATH: How would you know?

DANIELLE: I know.

KATH: He's probably disguised it. I mean, how stupid can you get, leaving your signature at the scene of a crime.

DANIELLE: I thought you said he was.

KATH: Was what?

DANIELLE: Stupid.

MO: Anyway, your dad painted over it.

KATH: One thing's for certain. I am never using Keaton's again.

(*PHYLLY enters with CRAIG, her in glamorous black, him in a cheap black suit.*)

PHYLLY: Look who's here. Little Craig McGellan.

I brought him in for a drink.

KATH: Where did you find him?

PHYLLY: Out front.

(*KATH reacts. MO intervenes.*)

MO: Why don't you have something to eat, Craig? You must be hungry after all your hard work.

KATH: He carried a coffin in and out of a church. How hard is that?

MO: Have a *vol au vent.*

KATH: I suppose I should be grateful he didn't drop it.

MO: (*To herself.*) Or tag it.

KATH: Have you invited anyone else while you were about it?

DANIELLE: Mum.

KATH: What about the other three pallbearers? The vicar? The grave diggers?

CRAIG: I better be off. Thanks for the drink.

PHYLLY: Thanks for the light.

(*CRAIG leaves, giving a conspiratorial wink at DAN-IELLE.*)

KATH: He's fourteen and you're encouraging him to smoke!

PHYLLY: Marijuana's not addictive.

KATH: If my front garden is full (of your butt ends.)

PHYLLY: (*Interrupting.*) Joke.

KATH: Not funny.

PHYLLY: Have you any idea how like Mum you sound? Oh, hi Danielle. How're you doing?

KATH: She's fine.

PHYLLY: Good. Does she speak yet?

MO: Let me get you a drink.

PHYLLY: Good old Mo. Always the peacemaker.

MO: How else would you two have survived?

(*PHYLLY laughs and hugs MO.*)

PHYLLY: How are all your little boys?

MO: Flown the nest. Only one left at home now. And he thinks I'm a chambermaid.

PHYLLY: So, what next? Cheers.

MO: Beats me. Don't suppose I'll stay on at the school once he leaves. Might get a job in a proper library.

KATH: If there are any left open.

PHYLLY: Oh it's good to be home.

KATH: This isn't home.

PHYLLY: I know but it feels like it. Mum upstairs, us all in the kitchen.

KATH: She's only visiting.

PHYLLY: Are you sure? She's showing all the signs of someone settling in for the duration.

KATH: Like a giant bloody cuckoo.

(*PHYLLY laughs.*)

It's all very well for you.

PHYLLY: How has she been?

KATH: Remarkably calm. Crisis seems to energise her. It's ordinary life she can't handle.

MO: Why doesn't she go and stay with you for a break in London?

KATH: Yes, why not? You're obviously doing very well for yourself. Got a good job? PA or something Dave said?

PHYLLY: It wouldn't be possible.

KATH: Oh? Why not?

PHYLLY: All her friends are here.

KATH: She hasn't got any friends.

PHYLLY: Oh come on.

KATH: They've either died or she's alienated them.

MO: She has become rather…

KATH: Rude

MO: Outspoken.

KATH: Depressed. I think some time with you would cheer her up, change of scene, bright lights. You two have always had so much to talk about. Now's your chance to catch up.

PHYLLY: It wouldn't work, I…

KATH: Why not?

PHYLLY: My job. It wouldn't be possible. The hours.

KATH: Oh come on. She took you in.

PHYLLY: I know that. (*Pours more wine.*) When I was a 'poor little scrap'. And then put up with me when I became rude and difficult…

KATH: So what's stopping you then?

PHYLLY: I wouldn't want to hurt her.

MO: How would you?

KATH: Phylly? What's happened?

PHYLLY: Nothing. I just don't see Mum sharing house room with my clients. Do you?

(*The others stare at her. PHYLLY shrugs.*)

PHYLLY: Buys nice clothes. Pays the rent. Not qualified to do much else. Santé.

KATH: All those...Isn't it...horrible?

PHYLLY: Just a job. Just men.

(*KATH goes to PHYLLY and puts her arms round her, kissing the top of her head.*
DAVE enters with an empty plate.)

DAVE: Okey dokey. Coming right up. Any more sandwiches girls?

MO: Go away.

(*Beat.*)

DAVE: Righto. (*Leaves.*)

PHYLLY: Poor man. He thought you were about to turn him to stone.

MO: I was.

DANIELLE: I wandered out into the road. Someone had tagged our front wall again. I climbed up, sat swinging my legs and waited for my father to appear out of the smoke and enfold me in his arms. Pan back. Freeze frame. Cut to credits. Even at fourteen, *The Railway Children* was still my favourite film. And why not hope? She'd come back. Why wouldn't he? And I'm still waiting. If I'd known then how long, maybe I wouldn't have, shouldn't have, bothered? (*Finds a tin/packet of biscuits and starts to eat as she remembers.*) You know something Striker once told me? He said the final and most painful scourge that crawled out of Pandora's box, after hatred and envy etc had been let out, was hope. I hoped for a little sister, a best friend and that my family would be just like everybody else's.

Scene 3

Spring 1978. Chronological order: Four.

DANIELLE: Those were the days when I still told my mother what had happened at school.

(*KATH's kitchen. MO watches as KATH stuffs the remains of DEREK's clothes into bags.*)

Mum. We did rectangles and there's a new girl and she had her Luke Skywalker confiscated too. D'you know what?

MO: Hello love.

DANIELLE: What're all the bags in the hall? Are we going on holiday?

MO: Kath?

(*KATH gives DANIELLE a strangling hug.*)

DANIELLE: And she gave me the kind of hug reserved for drowning people. Help! Mum!

MO: Kath, she can't breathe.

KATH: Sorry. I'm so sorry.

MO: Danielle why don't you play out the back for a while, till tea's ready?

DANIELLE: (*Watching her mother.*) I'm hungry now.

MO: Take a biscuit.

DANIELLE: Very hungry.

MO: Take two then.

DANIELLE: Starving.

MO: Go!

DANIELLE: And she bundled me out the back door with an entire tin of biscuits. Something was definitely going on in our house. Maybe Mum had won on the premium bonds and we were going to Disneyland Florida or even Butlins. That would explain the bags and the generosity with the biscuits. We were rich.

CRAIG: Stick em up.

(*DANIELLE holds the biscuit tin up in the air with both hands.*)

No. You Div. You give me the gold and then you stick them up.

DANIELLE: Sorry.

(*She hands him the tin and puts her hands in the air. CRAIG starts to eat the biscuits, ignoring DANIELLE whose arms begin to ache.*)

I know why Nicola Bunyan got sent to Miss Harrison. I saw her getting undressed for PE and she wouldn't take her sweater off and Miss said she had to and then Nicola Bunyan hid under her desk and swore.

CRAIG: She never.

DANIELLE: She did. Like this. (*Holds up two fingers in the peace sign.*)

CRAIG: Nicola Bunyan?

DANIELLE: Cross my heart and hope to die.

CRAIG: No. Her dad's got a BMW.

DANIELLE: And then anyway Miss made Nicola Bunyan come out and take off her sweater and then she had to see Miss Harrison cos she had measle burns on her arms.

CRAIG: Measles?

DANIELLE: Or something awful cos they made Miss cry out. She said OHMYGOD and then her eyes went red and she put Nicola Bunyan's sweater back on and took her to the Head. And we missed PE which wasn't fair cos today was apparatus with bean bags.

CRAIG: Let's play Dog Had.

DANIELLE: I'm not crawling round on my knees in my uniform. My mum'll kill me.

CRAIG: No, dumbo, it's just like Had only when you catch someone instead of saying Had. You say Dog Had.

DANIELLE: I knew that.

CRAIG: Liar.

DANIELLE: I did. And it's a stupid game.

CRAIG: Liar liar pants on fire.

DANIELLE: I'll get my dad on you.

CRAIG: So? My brothers'll sort him out.

DANIELLE: Leastways I got a dad.

CRAIG: No you haven't. He got caught playing away from home.

DANIELLE: I know that, he has a special bag. It's called badminton.

CRAIG: My mum said, everyone knows. And he's gone.

DANIELLE: Has not.

CRAIG: Has.

DANIELLE: Oh yes I remember. He's gone out to get tickets from Florida Disneyland.

CRAIG: Disneyland?

DANIELLE: He'll be back later.

CRAIG: We're having a baby sister.

DANIELLE: (*Envious.*) Ooh.

CRAIG: I'd rather have a dog but mum says I'll change my mind when it happens.

DANIELLE: I've always wanted a baby sister. I'd call her Linda or Leah. What're you going to call yours? (*CRAIG thinks for a moment.*)

CRAIG: Buster.

DANIELLE: You're telling lies Craig McGellan. You can't have a baby called Buster and you can't have a baby without a dad.

CRAIG: My mum can.

DANIELLE: And this is how I knew that Craig McGellan's mum was in fact the Virgin Mary. Or at least a close relation. A sister perhaps. Or maybe, like Aunt Phylly, Craig's sister came from another family altogether and was adopted. That would explain it. One day she'd just pop up as a surly three year old in a paddling pool scowling into the lens. I had nothing to envy. Did I?

I drew moustaches in my Wonder Woman scrapbook and felt better. (*Moves a pile of newspapers.*) Doesn't work any more. I wonder when it stopped being fun. Started it again in a desultory sort of way when I was fourteen and got glandular fever. I spent so much time lying on the sofa I became almost transparent. A backdrop to other people's actions. I was drifting around in a haze of diffused light, waiting for something or someone to pull me into focus. Not a lot's changed there then.

Scene 4

Summer 1988. Chronological order: Ten.

PHYLLY's garden. DANIELLE lies down on a lounger with her Walkman on as BRIAN wheels on a cast iron drinks trolley loaded with goodies.

BRIAN: Now, what'll you have. Maureen?

MO: Mo. Really. Erm well…

BRIAN: Bucks Fizz, Black Velvet? Or do you like your champagne neat?

MO: Who's driving?
(*She looks at DAVE who puts up his hand with a sigh.*)
Neat please.
BRIAN: What about Sleeping Beauty?
DANIELLE: Neat'll be grand for me an all.
BRIAN: They ruin your hearing you know those things.
DANIELLE: It's my English set book.
BRIAN: I'm sorry Phylly's mum couldn't come.
MO: She doesn't go anywhere much any more. She was never very sociable.
DANIELLE: Not like Grandad.
BRIAN: Is there nothing that can be done for her?
MO: She has anti-depressants.
DANIELLE: And Radio 4.
BRIAN: How worrying. Is it…you know…something that will pass on?
MO: Hereditary? No I don't think so.
BRIAN: Good.
(*DANIELLE rolls her eyes and goes back to listening to her Walkman.*)
DAVE: Thought you were supposed to be ill?
DANIELLE: I am. I'll be asleep in a minute.
DAVE: Keep on knocking back the booze and you'll be asleep all afternoon. Just a small beer thanks Brian.
DANIELLE: Good. I didn't want to come in the first place.
DAVE: What, and miss your auntie's house warming?
DANIELLE: Showing off.
DAVE: Seems like she's got plenty to show off.
(*PHYLLY and KATH enter. DANIELLE drinks her and DAVE'S champagne and helps herself to more when BRIAN's not looking.*)
BRIAN: Enjoy the guided tour?
KATH: Very nice.
BRIAN: My wife's become quite the expert on antiques. We haunt the auction rooms. David. (*Hands him a glass of champagne.*)
DAVE: Thanks but…
BRIAN: My wife's got such an eye for colour. I wanted to get a designer in – I mean the place was unspeakable when we bought it – but no, Phylly wanted to do it all herself.

DAVE: I'm into DIY too.

BRIAN: How interesting.

KATH: So, was it a big wedding then? Or just a few close family?

MO: Shall I hand these round?

BRIAN: We got married in Paris. On an impulse.

DAVE: We got married round the corner, on a Saturday.

MO: Dave.

DAVE: Everyone was there. All Mo's family, her best friends.

BRIAN: Ladies. (*He hands PHYLLY and KATH champagne.*) Reinforcements are required. (*Exits with the empty bottle.*)

DAVE: Oh Brian, while you're in the fridge, a beer would be terrific.

MO: You've already got champagne.

DAVE: (*Sitting down beside DANIELLE.*) Well I don't want it, makes me gassy.

MO: (*Turning her back on him.*) I don't know why you came. He'd have been far happier at home in front of the tele.

DANIELLE: I'll have your share.

DAVE: No you won't. How's the book?

DANIELLE: We're two down, ten minutes to the end of the first half.

(*DAVE takes one of the earpieces and he and DANIELLE listen in companionable silence.*)

MO: Where did you meet Brian?

PHYLLY: Through a friend.

KATH: He wasn't one of your…?

PHYLLY: Of course not.

KATH: Just asking.

PHYLLY: Far as my immediate past's concerned he's a little vague. However he knows I was adopted. We went to Somerset House. Checked everything out.

MO: I thought you got married on impulse?

PHYLLY: He needed to feel sure there were no skeletons in my cupboard.

KATH: This would be one of your antique cupboards would it?

PHYLLY: (*Giggling.*) Oh shut up. He needs to know where he is.

KATH: And where is he, on a scale of one to ten?

PHYLLY: Seven and a half.

MO: Seven and a half! (*Nodding at DAVE.*) If he's had a drink we don't even get to one.

PHYLLY: He is a bit older than Brian.

MO: Yes. Past his sell by date.

KATH: You've done all right for yourself then.

PHYLLY: Not before time.

MO: You're not are you?

PHYLLY: What? No. Not an option.

KATH: I'd have thought he'd make quite a good father. Not like Dada of course but…

PHYLLY: Well let's face it, no one would ever measure up to him. No wonder poor bloody Derek (left.)

MO: (*Interrupting.*) What about IVF or something?

PHYLLY: Wouldn't work.

KATH: Why?

PHYLLY: My own fault, bungled abortion. He doesn't know about that either, just thinks I'm too old. Not a word. Darling.
(*BRIAN enters with more champagne. At that moment DAVE's team scores. He leaps up, pulling the earpiece out of DANIELLE's ear.*)

DANIELLE: Ow.

DAVE: Yes!

BRIAN: Sorry, was I that long?
(*PHYLLY and KATH get the giggles. MO is annoyed and glares at DAVE.*)

DAVE: Sorry old thing.

BRIAN: Now, who's for a top up?

PHYLLY: Poor Danielle, you must be bored to death. Tell me what's happening in your life?

DANIELLE: Nothing much.

PHYLLY: How's that nice pallbearer friend of yours?

DANIELLE: (*Visibly brightening.*) Craig?

KATH: He's not a friend.

PHYLLY: I bet he's broken a few hearts already.

KATH: Actually his speciality's car windows.

DANIELLE: Mum.

KATH: He's in the family business. Vandalism. You know the sort.

PHYLLY: What sort's that?

KATH: McGellans. Trouble.

DANIELLE: Mum.

KATH: If there is one thing you can do for your kids, surely it's to make sure they don't make the same mistakes you did.

DANIELLE: He's not like that.

KATH: He's a McGellan. They run wild. Dada always said so.

BRIAN: Kath. For you?

(*KATH turns away to BRIAN.*)

Do try one of these. I ordered them specially, for Phylly's family.

DANIELLE: She never lets up. Once she gets something fixed in her head.

PHYLLY: I thought Craig was very charming.

DANIELLE: It's not his fault he doesn't have a dad.

PHYLLY: No. It's never the kid's fault.

DANIELLE: Whose is it then? God, fate, Mrs Thatcher?

(*Silence.*)

I mean it's always us who…you know…

PHYLLY: Miss out.

DANIELLE: Don't get me wrong. Mum's…. but yes – miss. Sometimes I just wish… you know, there was a proper reason.

PHYLLY: You think there is one?

DANIELLE: Fathers just don't go and never come back.

PHYLLY: Don't you see your dad at all?

DANIELLE: Occasionally. When he remembers. But it's not like he's a – he's there. Not like Grandad was.

I mean, oh fuckit.

PHYLLY: Are you all right?

KATH: What's going on?

DANIELLE: I'm okay. I'm going to be sick.

PHYLLY: Here.

(*PHYLLY grabs the ice bucket and DANIELLE turns away and is sick in it.*)

MO: It's not clever giving children alcohol.

DAVE: She's fourteen. She took it. They do.

MO: You really don't understand women at all do you?

KATH: Okay baby. Be all done in a minute.

DAVE: What've I done now?

MO: Oh nothing. As usual. (*Goes to join the women.*)

BRIAN: Looks like you're in the doghouse, David my old son.

DAVE: I'm there so often these days I'm thinking of having it redecorated. D'you think Phylly might give me a hand with the colour scheme?

MO: Come on love. We'll find you some mouthwash.

PHYLLY: Nearest bathroom's at the top of the stairs on the right

KATH: What did you say to her?

PHYLLY: She wanted to know about Derek. Just trying to find someone to blame I suppose.

KATH: Well it wasn't my fault.

(*The sisters' eyes meet.*
DANIELLE looks at a photo in a frame of her and Striker deciding who it belongs to. Places it face down.)

DANIELLE: Fault always suggests to me a great gaping rift down the middle of something. We had that. I should have seen the signs. I could have checked where he was playing away. You can always find out if you want to.

I don't think it's stupid to keep hoping. Not until you know what you want to do about it. (*Zips up the kitbag and puts it firmly to one side.*)

Scene 5

Summer 1978. Chronological order: Five.

DANIELLE: My fourth summer smelled of lemonade and cut grass. For months after he left I was in a state of permanent alert for my father's return. I scanned the hall on a daily basis. It got so's I could become over excited by the sight of a Sainsbury's carrier bag left propped against the radiator. He could have just gone shopping and got hit by amnesia. A kind lady with streaked blonde hair and an estate car had loaded him in the back and taken him to hospital where he'd remained incognito until suddenly the sound of a young girl's voice – bearing an uncanny resemblance to mine – had woken him from his trance and he'd rushed home still clutching his carrier bag of by now rotten food.

I'd run into the kitchen, arms wide, truly believing I'd find him there, in sepia tones, sat at the table, drinking tea with my mother who'd be telling him how his wonderful daughter could now not only do rectangles but rhomboids also, all coloured in without going over the lines. And he'd swing me up and round and his chin would be prickly and his neck all smelling of his smell that was his alone. And he'd hug me tight as a bug in a rug and tell me he was never going away again, not even to badminton or Sainsbury's. (*Runs into the kitchen with her satchel to see a stranger sitting at the table with her mother. She stops and stares at him.*)

KATH: Hello love. Did Mo just drop you off? How was your day?

DANIELLE: The shutters closed. Opened again. He was still there.

KATH: Aren't you going to say hello to our guest? Felix comes from South Africa.
(*DANIELLE glares at him.*)

FELIX: Hi Danielle. Pleased to meet you.

KATH: I'm afraid my daughter seems to have forgotten her manners. I promise you, she had them when she went out this morning.
(*KATH laughs nervously. FELIX doesn't get the joke.*)

FELIX: I expect she's not used to having strange men sitting in her kitchen.

DANIELLE: My mother's eyes darted me a warning. One wrong move and I could see bed without TV galloping towards me over the horizon.

KATH: I expect you're just hungry. What d'you want to eat?

DANIELLE: Whiskas.

KATH: I beg your pardon?

DANIELLE: My friend has a cat called Felix.

FELIX: Ah yes?

DANIELLE: She says they couldn't afford the vet so her father took its bollocks off in their greenhouse with a pair of pliers.

KATH: Danielle out.

DANIELLE: But I'm hungry.

KATH: To your room.

FELIX: I guess I ought to be going anyway.

DANIELLE: Can't I watch TV?

(*KATH glares at her. DANIELLE shrugs.*)

Sometimes you just have to try and cheat destiny, even when you can hear the clink of its bridle and feel its hot breath moistening the hairs on your neck. Time to climb into the saddle and head on up to bed with no supper and no TV. (*With satisfaction.*) And no Felix. (*Looking around her, the satisfaction disappears. She gets an asprin and swallows it with a glass of wine.*) It would seem I'm quite good at getting people to go away. Destiny or desire? Striker says I don't want commitment. I claim he jumped. He says he was pushed. Must be how you see it. After all everyone leaves sooner or later. Don't they?

Scene 6

Summer 1988. Chronological order: Eleven.

DANIELLE: The night my grandmother died our family landscape changed again. The angle of view skewed sideways by the manner of her departure. I suppose she'd been rehearsing for it ever since my Grandad went, inhabiting a shadowy world full of imagined enemies, demons and judges, never going out unless medically necessary. Not knowing that tonight was the night however, we carried on with our lives as if the sun would rise for us all the following day. Meanwhile alone in her room upstairs, leaning her head back against the antimacassar that her mother had crocheted, my grandmother sipped and swallowed the contents of three bottles of pills. Two were in combination lethal. The third – laxatives – she added for good measure, like a cook throwing in an extra handful of her favourite ingredient. Why that night rather than another? Was it raining then too? She had long fingers, the skin on her hands loose and cool. Did her hands shake, that night when the unthinkable became possible and the undoable was done? (*DANIELLE does her homework on the sofa while MO, KATH and PHYLLY follow a yoga video on the TV.*)

MO: I hate cooking, I hate cleaning, washing, ironing, hairs in the plughole, drips on the rim, rings on the collar, scum round the bath.

PHYLLY: That's why you're coming on the climb. We're going to leave all that behind.

KATH: You'll have to cook sometime.

PHYLLY: Heating up tins, that's okay, like camping.

MO: I hate camping.

KATH: Oh I wish I could see this.

PHYLLY: It's not too late to join us.

KATH: How could I? I couldn't. Even if I wanted to.

PHYLLY: Brian hasn't paid for the flights yet.

KATH: I can't see him wanting to fork out for another one.

PHYLLY: He'll write it off against tax and his company's already getting benefits from the publicity.

KATH: What, that article in the journal with you two waving your sponsorship forms? 'LOCAL WOMEN TO CLIMB MOUNT KILIMANJARO.'

PHYLLY: It's true. The caring face of capitalism.

MO: It's not just home. Everything annoys me. It's got so I resent the kids coming into the library because they'll mess up my shelves. I seem to spend my life putting things in order so other people can throw them about again. Like Hercules shovelling shit all day and never getting anywhere – except without all those muscles.

PHYLLY: Don't knock muscles, they're going to come in very handy.

MO: Why? We are just walking aren't we? I'm not doing anything with ropes and clingons.

PHYLLY: Crampons.

MO: Nor those. Walk up a mountain you said, raise lots of money for charity and have a week away from home. It'll be fun, you said.

KATH: With her, in a tent?

PHYLLY: It will be. An adventure.

KATH: We did tents in Spain, remember?

PHYLLY: Brandy at the gasolinera at seven am.

KATH: Sand in your teeth, your hair.

MO: Your crotch.

KATH: Did you?

PHYLLY: Sleeping under the stars.

KATH: Only when you were too drunk to find the tent.

MO: We slept on lilos, didn't we?

KATH: Mine had a puncture. I was so tired on the coach going home I slept through all the mealstops, missed France entirely and woke up at Victoria.

MO: I know. You were supposed to be keeping me company. Where was she?

KATH: She'd gone off hitching with those German lads.

MO: Weren't they Australian?

KATH: That was Jersey when we worked in that café. The lifeguard with the wife and baby.

PHYLLY: He didn't tell me about them till afterwards.

KATH: When his wife wrote to Mum. Remember? And Dada said Phylly'd either got to marry him or give him up altogether.

PHYLLY: As they'd already gone back to Australia it wasn't exactly a hard choice. Oh come on, come with us. It'll be brilliant. It'll change your life.

KATH: I like my life.

PHYLLY: Be a challenge.

KATH: You've run out of rooms to redecorate. You should try looking after mum, working down the shop and bringing up a teenage daughter single handed for a challenge.
(*PHYLLY mimes violin playing.*)
    Oh shut up.

PHYLLY: Don't be such a burnt chop. Danielle will be gone soon anyway. Then what'll you do?
(*The video starts to talk them through relaxation exercises lying flat on their backs.*)

KATH: No she won't. She's got three more years at school. After that she won't be able to afford to live anywhere but home and go to college. And Mum'll go on for ever. Outlive us all.

PHYLLY: How is she?

KATH: Don't ask. I could do Mastermind on the subject of her colon. Is this really supposed to relax you?

DANIELLE: I think you're meant to concentrate.

KATH: Oh.

DANIELLE: You know, like in silence.
(*Silence.*)
PHYLLY: When's your concert again?
MO: Thursday.
PHYLLY: Got any sponsors from the choir?
MO: Only Theo.
PHYLLY: Theo?
MO: Theo Hawes.
PHYLLY: He's the one you're doing the duet with?
KATH: The young one.
MO: Yes.
KATH: With the magical voice.
MO: Yes.
PHYLLY: The one you fancy.
MO: Yes. No. He's got a lovely voice.
KATH: Magical.
PHYLLY: Married?
MO: No.
KATH: Since when's that worried you?
PHYLLY: This isn't me we're talking about.
MO: It's no big deal. He's just fun that's all. We sing well
    together.
    (*The others look at her.*)
    He doesn't call me Old Thing or expect me to pick up
    his socks. He talks to me about Handel and Monteverdi.
    His stomach is flat and he rides a bike. He's got a tan that
    doesn't end at his neck and he bites his nails.
PHYLLY: Euch. I hate bitten nails. Don't you? Sorry.
    I interrupted.
KATH: What're you going to do?
MO: Nothing. This is Mo remember. Old Faithful. Wife and
    mother. My boys'd never forgive me. I'm just dreaming.
DANIELLE: I can see now it had never occurred to me till
    then that parents worried about what us kids thought
    about them. Certainly didn't seem of much account in my
    family. I know I felt really sorry for Dave. He was a bit of
    an old fogey but at least he stuck around. He came into
    my category of Safe Dads, alongside Richard Briers, Phil
    Archer and knitting patterns. The sort who never let you

down – with big hands and check vyella shirts. The second most preferred Group was Film Star Dad. I sat beside him during screenings of his latest movie. Everyone else would be looking at the screen watching him making people laugh, cry, fall in love with him but I'd have the real thing right beside me in the dark. And he'd look down at me and squeeze my hand and say 'Do you like it? That's all that matters to me.' Rock Star Father came third and his group were much younger and a bit ambivalent. They were glamorous, sexy and took me everywhere with them on tour. Beautiful girls would hang about the stage door but Rock Star Dad would prefer to go out after the gig with me on his arm. Girls were two a penny but his daughter was special. If ever proof were needed that I was held firmly in the jaws of adolescence, Rock Star Father was it. Freddie Mercury, I miss you. But even dead legends couldn't compete with the real life immediate anguish that was Craig McGellan, at that time to be seen draped around the pale, cigarette scarred shoulders of my best friend Nicola Bunyan. Sex, death and pain, the three horsemen of adolescence – and your twenties. Well, so far anyway. Surely it doesn't go on for ever. They do say it runs in families. That once it's close to you suicide becomes…familiar. Becomes, how shall I say…an option. It was Mo who came to take care of us. I don't know how she knew.

Scene 7

Summer 1988. Chronological order: Twelve.

KATH's living room/kitchen.

MO: (*Entering.*) I'm so sorry love.
DANIELLE: Thanks.
MO: It was so sudden. I had no idea…
DANIELLE: I know. Me neither.
MO: I came straight round.
DANIELLE: How did you find out?
MO: You rang me, don't you remember?
DANIELLE: I didn't. Did I?

(*KATH and PHYLLY enter. PHYLLY carries a bottle of brandy and a toothmug.*)

PHYLLY: Hello Mo. We're orphans.

KATH: You're not. You've probably still got a father roaming about out there somewhere. Whoever he is.

PHYLLY: You always say just the right thing. How d'you do that?

MO: (*Hugging them both.*) I'm so sorry.

KATH: Don't you think it's a little early for any more of that?

PHYLLY: No. Actually I don't. In fact on the list of jolly good reasons for having a drink before breakfast, I'd say one's mother topping herself in your spare room would come pretty high. Wouldn't you?

KATH: It wasn't your spare room. It was mine.

PHYLLY: Silly me. That makes it all right then. Would you like some?

MO: No thanks.

PHYLLY: It's good stuff. Only the best for Brian. He's earned it. He deserves it. Did I tell you he was brought up by his grandmother? Dead now too. She was so afraid of something happening to him, when he went on a plane, she'd buy a ticket too so if it crashed, they'd die together. He must have had some dreadful holidays.

KATH: You're going to feel dreadful too later.

PHYLLY: Always delay pain. That's my motto. By the time it catches up with you, with any luck, you're somewhere else entirely.

(*MO goes to sit with DANIELLE, arm around her.*)

MO: Who's up there now?

PHYLLY: God. Probably. Possibly. Depending on your point of view.

MO: No, upstairs.

KATH: They're taking her…away. There's got to be a post mortem.

PHYLLY: In case Kath killed her by stuffing her full of laxatives.

MO: What?

KATH: Mum swallowed everything she could find.

PHYLLY: They worked too. Hell of an advert. Keeps you regular even after…

(*They are interrupted by CRAIG in a black suit.*)

CRAIG: Excuse me. We're just taking your...Mrs Bradshaw now.

(*KATH glares at him.*)

If you'd call Mr Keaton tomorrow, about the arrangements.

PHYLLY: Thank you Craig. You did that very nicely.

(*CRAIG smiles sympathetically at DANIELLE before he and the undertaker carry Gran out.*)

MO: I'll help you clear up, shall I?

PHYLLY: All yesterday evening we were sitting down here.

KATH: She knew we were sitting down here.

PHYLLY: Didn't you say goodnight when you went up?

KATH: It was one o'clock. Her light was out.

PHYLLY: Didn't you hear anything?

KATH: Such as?

PHYLLY: I don't know. There should have been some sound. Something... stopping.

(*DANIELLE suddenly starts to cry. KATH hurries to her.*)

KATH: Now look what you've done. Oh love I'm sorry. I know. You'll miss her. It's a shock for all of us.

DANIELLE: (*Gulping between sobs.*) It's not fair.

PHYLLY: I know. Poor Danny.

DANIELLE: (*Sobbing.*) I wish I was dead. I haven't got any mascara on and my hair's filthy dirty.

(*KATH and PHYLLY exchange worried glances.*)

PHYLLY: I'm sure mum wouldn't have minded.

DANIELLE: Why did it have to be him? Why couldn't they have just sent someone else?

(*Laughing and crying at once, PHYLLY hugs DAN-IELLE.*)

Such pain. And adults look at you and go, you'll get over it. But you don't. It just becomes part of your baggage. And everywhere you go you take it with you. A whole photo library of feelings. Carvings in your bones. (*Looks around her.*) In my family the women don't seem to travel light.

Scene 8

Summer 1988. Chronological order: Thirteen.

Outside, a hill. KATH, PHYLLY, MO and DANIELLE enter carrying a picnic bag, rugs, fold up chairs and a designer label smart paper carrier bag.

KATH: This is far enough, surely?

PHYLLY: You're out of condition.

KATH: I'm just thinking of Danielle.

PHYLLY: She's fine. Aren't you Danny?

KATH: She won't be if she has a relapse.

MO: What a lovely day for it. And what a beautiful spot. Isn't it warm? I'm going to take off a layer. Aren't you hot Phylly?

PHYLLY: Mo?

MO: Yes?

PHYLLY: D'you have an off button?

KATH: So, are we agreed we're stopping here then?

MO: Here love, you sit on this.

(*DANIELLE moves the blanket into the shade.*)

DANIELLE: I'm going in the shade.

KATH: Take a drink with you.

DANIELLE: I'm not thirsty. (*Lies apart, tearing the petals off daisies, doing 'He loves me/not'.*)

PHYLLY: Do stop clucking.

KATH: The child has had glandular fever.

MO: I know this is a tense time for you both…

PHYLLY: Mo!

KATH: Mo!

MO: Okay then, you get on with it. (*Hands over a Sainsbury's bag.*) Handbag, sandwiches. (*Passes the smart carrier.*) Mother.

DANIELLE: What d'you mean?

KATH: She's got to go sometime.

DANIELLE: You mean you're going to dump her here?

PHYLLY: No, we thought she might like the outing.

MO: Phylly!

PHYLLY: I'm sorry. But really.

KATH: Not dump. Scatter. It's what people usually do.

MO: You could put her round the roses if you'd rather.

DANIELLE: We haven't got any roses.

PHYLLY: I've got a whole walk of them at my place.

KATH: No.

PHYLLY: Didn't think you'd go for that.

MO: You could bury them.

PHYLLY: A friend of mine who had a scare recently left instructions that a spoonful of her ashes were to be sent to each of her friends and relations in an envelope. Didn't open the post over breakfast for weeks.

KATH: Are you trying to be offensive or can you just not help it?

MO: Why don't we leave your Mum where she is for now. It's such a nice day.

PHYLLY: Implication being if it weren't we'd just tip her out and be done with it?

KATH: I'm going home.

PHYLLY: No don't. I'm sorry. Kath! Really. I'll behave.

KATH: Now when have I heard that before? Like all my life.

PHYLLY: This time I mean it. Promise. Come on, let's do the handbag. Please?
(*KATH takes the bag out of the carrier.*)

MO: I wonder why she didn't leave a note.

PHYLLY: Or a will.

MO: You've been to the bank?
(*KATH gives her a look, of course she has.*)
 Sorry.

KATH: Apart from her bits of furniture, clothes, her wedding ring and a couple of hundred pounds – this is it. I've cleaned out all the drawers. Everything.

PHYLLY: Ooh look. Baby photos. (*Picks out a small pocketbook of snapshots.*)

MO: Why do we always take pictures of our kids with chocolate or ice cream all over their faces?

KATH: And daft hats.

MO: Hundreds when we're little and none when we're old?

DANIELLE: Cos old people are boring. They don't change. Kids do.

PHYLLY: You're right, look, chocolate. Mum had those dresses made specially.

MO: Whatever happened to seersucker?

KATH: That was my wetting doll you've got there.

PHYLLY: How do you remember these things?

KATH: There's me newborn.

PHYLLY: Did you take an inventory?

(*They are suddenly silent as they turn the page and see a very old dogeared shot.*)

MO: Oh my God.

KATH: Why did she keep that?

DANIELLE: (*Coming over to look.*) What?

PHYLLY: Me at three. Never know my hair was blonde would you?

DANIELLE: (*Shocked.*) You look…

PHYLLY: Could have used me on posters.

KATH: Why would she keep that?

PHYLLY: I think I came with it.

KATH: But why keep it?

PHYLLY: Encouragement she could only do better?

DANIELLE: Have you still got those marks?

PHYLLY: They faded. Hardly show now. Living proof older people do change. (*Beat.*) Right what else have we got in here? Post office book, kirby grips, ear rings – paste, shame. Postcard from Tarragona. 'Having a lovely time, met a V fab German boy. Very brown. Love Kath.' (*Looks at KATH.*) 'V fab German boy?' What happened to him? (*KATH shrugs.*)

MO: He went off hitchhiking.

PHYLLY: Really? (*Penny drops.*) Ah. You weren't really serious about him?

KATH: His name was Wolfram. He was going to show me Salzburg.

MO: Wolfram Kock. I remember now.

PHYLLY: Oh come on, Mrs Kock?

KATH: It was Köck – with an umlaut.

MO: It was a long time ago.

PHYLLY: Nothing happened.

KATH: There were so many, how would you remember?

PHYLLY: I'm sure it didn't. With or without the umlaut. (*Beat. Looks at the handbag contents.*) So, that's the lot.

KATH: Not much is it, for a lifetime?

MO: She had you two, three.

KATH: And Dada.

PHYLLY: Sun's gone in. Shall we go back?

(*They pack up.*)

MO: We never had our picnic.

PHYLLY: Come on the climb with us Kath. You've no reason not to now.

KATH: I've plenty – there's fitness, heights, insects, tents. And that's just off the top of my head.

PHYLLY: It'd be better this time, I promise.

KATH: And how exactly could it be worse?

PHYLLY: It'll be good for you.

KATH: What about Danielle, the shop, I've got responsibilities?

PHYLLY: It can all be arranged.

DANIELLE: I could stay with a friend.

MO: Dave would have her.

KATH: I don't do that sort of thing.

PHYLLY: Why not?

KATH: Because.

PHYLLY: What?

KATH: Because if you really want to know, I think it's just silly and attention seeking.

PHYLLY: You're scared of making a fool of yourself.

KATH: Well exactly. Grown women cavorting about in big boots and shorts.

PHYLLY: If we wear trousers will you come?

KATH: Don't be stupid.

MO: Slingbacks?

KATH: (*Laughing.*) I don't want to do it. I don't want anything else to happen. I don't need shaking up. I want everything to go back to how it was.

MO: How it was when?

KATH: I don't know.

DANIELLE: Childhood? The time before Christmas went wrong? Or maybe it was when they were happy, her and Dad.

But was she happy the same time he was? I sometimes think if humans were meant to live in couples, they'd surely have got some kind of mate-for-life gene, like swans. (*Picks up a pile of old jazz records and drops them into a packing case.*) His.

Scene 9

Summer 1978. Chronological order: Six.

DANIELLE: After my father left my mother didn't go out often but when she did she'd drop me at Mo's where I'd be put to bed head to toe with one of her boys who slept stacked in bunks. I never stayed there long but was usually discovered later – still life of sleeping child – on the stairs. Like a piece of left luggage. Waiting and watching through the gaps in other people's lives. (*Sits on the stairs watching DAVE and MO who are sewing name tapes on school uniform.*)

MO: It's not going to be easy. She's never even looked at anyone else since she met Derek.

DAVE: Oh come on. You three were at it like knives in those days.

MO: We weren't. Phylly maybe.

DAVE: Nothing changes.

MO: I wish she was here now.

DAVE: You miss her?

MO: She needed to go…but… Just bad timing really. How could Derek just leave? I'd die if you left me and the boys.

DAVE: I'm not going to.

MO: You could have been a famous archeologist by now if it weren't for us, travelling the world, writing books.

DAVE: Or I could have failed my finals, had that nervous breakdown I was headed for and be on my third marriage.

MO: Third?

DAVE: Is this about me or Derek?

MO: He had a baby. Didn't stop him running off with a bleached blonde with an ace serve and a Volvo estate.

DAVE: Yeah, the Volvo is tempting.

MO: Kath says he never wanted children.

DAVE: Lot of men don't till they get them.

MO: And we have to take that risk?

DAVE: All of it's a risk. In the end, you have to go by instinct and you have to be brave.

MO: Do you really love me?

DAVE: Course I do. D'you think I'd be sitting here sewing on bloody name tapes if I didn't? (*Kisses her.*) Oh fuck the name tapes. If they don't know who they are by now… (*They kiss more passionately.*)

MO: (*Coming up for air.*) Will it always be this good?

DAVE: Course. (*Grinning.*) How the hell should I know? You worry too much. That's what the boys have done for you.

MO: Don't you ever worry?

DAVE: Why bother when you do it so well?

MO: (*Affectionately.*) Bastard.

DAVE: You ought to go out more.

MO: Out costs money.

DAVE: Join something. Have fun. What about a choir?

MO: No. I can't sing. Not anymore.

DAVE: You used to be always singing. Remember?

MO: That was before I had kids.

DAVE No. You sang to them. What was it? Something like. I know…(*Sings.*) You are my sunshine,

MO: No.

DAVE: Yes. (*Sings.*) My only sunshine… Come on.
(*MO joins in. She has a beautiful voice. DAVE harmonises.*)

MO: (*Singing.*) My only sunshine.
You make me happy when skies are grey.
You'll never know dear how much I love you.
Please don't take my sunshine away.
(*DAVE does the banjo plink plonk sounds, speeding them up into the repeat verse.*)

DANIELLE: That was it. As surely as the shaft of yellow streetlight shining onto the stairs held me in its spotlight. I knew. It was at that moment. Mum had said he never wanted me. They were all right till I came along. It was my fault he'd left! It felt so cold out there. And they looked as warm and cosy as a Christmas card.

MO/DAVE: You'll never know dear how much I love you.
Please don't take my sunshine away.

End of Act One.

ACT TWO

DANIELLE divides up books, putting one pile into an old kit bag.

DANIELLE: Striker says I don't engage. I just stand on the sidelines of life. His metaphor not mine. Observing. But it's what I do. Look, frame, focus, hold, shoot. And if you're lucky you get something that's bigger than the picture you took. And if you're even luckier and someone's paying you, you get Second Elevens and Stout Mayoral visits and dazed Centenarians clutching their telegrams. Oh it was definitely worth living all those years for this, wasn't it Gran? Fuck off and give us a port and lemon. It's what I do. Years of practice? Maybe. If I was someone different I'd restore vintage cars and in my spare time chase a ball around a wet field shouting Man On. And another one bites the dust. Packing up the past. I wish I felt sad, not just tired.

Scene 1

Summer 1988. Chronological order: Fourteen.

PHYLLY and KATH are circuit training in PHYLLY's garden. DANIELLE has the stop watch and is overseeing them. KATH is hugely out of condition. She attempts sit-ups while PHYLLY does star jumps. DANIELLE has an old kit bag beside her.

PHYLLY: It's probably in your attic.

KATH: How would it get there?

DANIELLE: Mum, if you can talk and do sit ups you're not doing them right.

PHYLLY: Maybe you put it out with the rubbish by mistake. (*DANIELLE's stop watch beeps.*)

DANIELLE: Move to the next station.

KATH: I don't throw things away by accident. I don't throw things away at all if I can help it, least of all my mother's ashes.

DANIELLE: Mum, move on.

KATH: I am not doing that. I draw the line at skipping.

DANIELLE: Skip that one and do press ups then.

KATH: You are joking.

DANIELLE: Look either you want to get fit or you don't.

KATH: Actually I don't particularly.

PHYLLY: I'll do them with you.

KATH: How will that help?

PHYLLY: Competition?

(*They start their press-ups. KATH is hopeless.*)

DANIELLE: Put your hands under your shoulders.

PHYLLY: How's your sponsorship going?

KATH: Quite a few customers have signed my list. None are paying up front though I've noticed.

DANIELLE: Come on, three and four.

KATH: Mo's late.

PHYLLY: I wonder what made you think of her at this precise moment.

(*KATH laughs and collapses.*)

DANIELLE: Mum, you're not trying.

KATH: She made me laugh.

DANIELLE: Where is Mo?

PHYLLY: Erm. Choir practice?

DANIELLE: No we arranged it so they wouldn't clash.

PHYLLY: I expect she'll be along later. Kath?

KATH: (*Face down on the mat.*) No. I can't do this. I'm too old.

DANIELLE: You have to keep going.

(*BRIAN enters with a box.*)

Come on, just two more.

BRIAN: Don't lift your hips. Keep your back straight. No no no. Like this. (*Demonstrates with agility.*) See? Can you see the difference?

KATH: I can see how easy you find it, Brian. But how does that help me exactly?

BRIAN: Watch Phylly then. Go on, do it again. Don't drop your head. Better. She's got the hang of it. Nearly.

KATH: Maybe you'd like to go instead of me?

BRIAN: Love to. Can't afford the time. I leave the charity work to you girls. On the subject of which. Tracksuits.

(*Opens the box he's brought in and pulls out a brightly coloured tracksuit top with a large dayglow fish on the front and* SUPERFISH *emblazoned on the back.*) What d'you think? Kath?

KATH: Very…colourful.

PHYLLY: I thought we were just going to have the logo sort of, on the shoulder. (*Sketches a little box to show the size she'd anticipated.*)

BRIAN: No point in advertising if you can't see it.

KATH: Where from, the air?

BRIAN: Good point. Safety factor. Visibility.

KATH: Well, they won't miss us in these.

(*MO enters looking flushed.*)

BRIAN: Try them on. Aha. The third musketeer. There you go.

MO: Thank you. What's this? Sorry I'm late.

BRIAN: Are you limping?

MO: I pulled a muscle.

BRIAN: That won't do. Not at this stage of the game. I'll send you to my physio. She'll sort you out.

KATH: I think that's already been done.

BRIAN: Go on, try it on then.

MO: Right.

BRIAN: You got dressed in a hurry. Sweater's on back to front.

KATH: (*Muttering as she gets into the hideous tracksuit.*) I'm not wearing this.

PHYLLY: Humour him. He's paying.

KATH: You humour him. He's your husband.

PHYLLY: It was part of the deal.

KATH: Not mine.

PHYLLY: He gets to advertise.

KATH: And we get to look like Koi Carp with bosoms. Terrific.

(*DANIELLE is trying to hide her amusement.*)

BRIAN: There's one for you too Danielle, as their 'coach'. Wouldn't want you to feel left out.

DANIELLE: Thanks Brian.

BRIAN: If I were you I'd try it on.

PHYLLY: (*Warning KATH.*) Don't say one word.

DANIELLE: I'm sure it'll be fine.

BRIAN: I'll put it in your bag then. Otherwise you'll go off without it. I know you. Leave it lying around, some people will nick anything.

MO: They'd have to be bloody desperate to steal these.

DANIELLE: (*Grabbing the track suit from BRIAN.*) No. It's all right. I'll do it.

PHYLLY: Pulled a muscle eh?

MO: Getting out the car.

KATH: You did it in the car?

MO: No. I was outside his place getting my bag out the boot and suddenly it went. Of course I had to pretend nothing was the matter.

PHYLLY: Why?

MO: I couldn't exactly limp into the love nest could I?

PHYLLY: How was it?

MO: Typical bachelor's room – not unlike my Steven's.

PHYLLY: Not the décor. It.

MO: Well I think he was happy cos I kept shouting with what he thought was pleasure. I didn't let on it was actually shooting pains like fireworks up my left buttock.

PHYLLY: How's it now?

MO: Agony.

BRIAN: Right then. Let's have a photo. In a row.

KATH: Shouldn't we lie head to tail?

MO: I tell you one thing, I'll never make a masochist.

BRIAN: Smile for the camera.

(*They do. The others leave. DANIELLE shoves a kitbag into the understairs cupboard.*)

DANIELLE: His.

Scene 2

Autumn 1978. Chronological order: Seven.

Under the stairs at KATH's.

CRAIG: Sardines?

DANIELLE: You get in a hiding place all together and hide from each other.

CRAIG: In the same place?

DANIELLE: Yeah. Sort of. Like cupboards and that. Like here, under the stairs. My mum used to play it when she was little. In the olden days.

CRAIG: There's no kissing is there?

DANIELLE: (*Lying.*) No Craig, course not.

CRAIG: You sure? Only I don't do kissing.

DANIELLE: (*Aside.*) Another gameplan gone awry.
(*To CRAIG.*) If you don't want to play...

CRAIG: I do. So, who gets to look for us then?

DANIELLE: (*Improvising.*) The dad. He comes home from the badminton and searches high and low.

CRAIG: Is he looking for me too?

DANIELLE: Oh yes. He loves children.
(*Beat.*)

CRAIG: Well then, when's he coming?

DANIELLE: Soon. (*Beat.*) When the sport's over.

CRAIG: Ssh.
(*KATH comes downstairs with a carrier bag, followed by MO.*)

MO: Come on, how much?

KATH: They were on offer.

MO: Show.

KATH: What d'you think?

MO: Lovely.

KATH: You hate them.

MO: No. They're just, well just like all the others you've got.

KATH: Not the colour.

MO: What did she say this time? Come on, it goes words with your mum, shopping spree, remorse – closely followed by debt.

KATH: This time she said he never takes her out anywhere. I mean like she'd go. No wonder none of my friends ever wanted to come back to ours.

MO: They did. Well, I did.

KATH: Why did you?

MO: Something was always going on here.

KATH: Like Mum going manic.

MO: It didn't happen that often. In fact I only remember the once. When she barricaded herself into the understairs cupboard.

KATH: Don't.

MO: It was Phylly got her out wasn't it?

KATH: Probably. Saint Phyllida's responsible for most of the miracles round here. Shame she's had to remove her magic powers back to London just when they could have come in handy.

MO: She was always wild.

KATH: D'you think she sees Derek?

MO: London's a big place.

KATH: Suppose so.

MO: Have you heard from him?

KATH: No just the solicitor.

(*MO steels herself to say something.*)

What?

MO: I got a letter from Phylly this morning.

KATH: With an address?

MO: Yes but…

KATH: Thank goodness for that. Dada was beginning to think something had happened to her. I keep telling him she'll be fine, she's just getting settled, but anyway, now he'll be able to contact her.

MO: She had some news.

KATH: What?

MO: About Derek.

KATH: Oh my God, he's dead?

(*Before MO can answer there's a scream from the under-stairs cupboard. They run to open it.*)

Danielle!

(*KATH pulls out a terrified CRAIG. DANIELLE is screaming.*)

What did you do to her?

CRAIG: Nothing. I didn't do nothing!

KATH: What are you doing in here?

CRAIG: Let me go. We was just playing fathers that's all.

MO: Come on Danny out you come.

KATH: Fathers! If you've touched her…

CRAIG: You're hurting me!

MO: Kath let go of him.

KATH: Get out. I don't want to see you here again. I'll be round to talk to your mother later.

CRAIG: I don't care. It's a stupid game anyway. Cos my dad's never coming to find me. (*Exits.*)

DANIELLE: (*Sobbing.*) Nor's mine.

KATH: They've been listening.

MO: No hang on love. Derek's not dead.

KATH: He's not? Danielle ssh.

MO: No, I was trying to tell you. He's getting married.

KATH: (*Sitting down suddenly.*) Oh shit.

MO: Look at it this way. You're free now.

KATH: (*Looking at DANIELLE.*) With his face looking at me every day? I don't think so.

DANIELLE: It wasn't my fault I looked like him, was it? We never played in the understairs cupboard again. For one thing Mum filled it full of all the exercise bikes and rowing machines she'd bought to get in shape. For another Craig wasn't allowed over the doorstep. Neither was Dad come to that. Not that he tried very hard. He came one Saturday and took me out to the park but it rained and we had to go to the cinema for the afternoon, after which I had serial nightmares and took up sleepwalking and she said never again. He wasn't fit. In his absence however the images, like the toys in the cupboard, took on a life of their own. All men wore my father's face – from the newscaster on TV to the armed robber photofit outside the police station. He was everywhere and nowhere. Like trying to put your arms round mist.

Scene 3

Late summer 1988. Chronological order: Fifteen.

MO and KATH enter with backpacks, stout boots etc.

MO: Oh my God look at that view.

KATH: We must be getting fitter.

MO: Why must we?

KATH: Listen to our breathing. We've just climbed a thousand foot hill complete with backpacks and we can still speak. (*PHYLLY and DANIELLE enter.*)

PHYLLY: There. I knew we could do it. Give us your hand. And it's not raining. What more could we ask?

KATH: A sunset.

MO: Tea. I'm famished.

DANIELLE: A fire.

KATH: Tent first.

MO: (*Standing to attention.*) Sarge major!

KATH: I'm just saying. We don't want to be doing this in the dark.

MO: We may have to when we do the real thing.

PHYLLY: Okay. We've done it in the back garden, here's no different.

MO: Except for the mist. We're not going to see any sunset at this rate.

KATH: Let's just get on with it.

(*They start to unpack parts of the tent.*)

PHYLLY: Danny do you want to call out?

DANIELLE: Not much.

PHYLLY: Shall I then?

KATH: Go ahead.

MO: I've got the poles.

KATH: Don't we do the tent first?

PHYLLY: Yes. Lay it out flat.

KATH: Pull your side, Mo.

PHYLLY: Okay. Who's got the fly? Oh. I have. Fine, now the poles.

(*As they talk the women efficiently put up the tent.*)

KATH: When you were small Danielle you had a little A frame tent. D'you remember? We put it up in the sitting room for your birthday.

DANIELLE: There was a photo,wasn't there, later on? With me and Gran in it? In the back garden.

KATH: She'd just come out of hospital, said sleeping under the sky would be the best possible antidote.

DANIELLE: And you let her?

KATH: I was on the sofa in the sitting room with the back door open all night. You were only about five feet away.

PHYLLY: Okay, thread them through.

DANIELLE: Where was my dad?

KATH: Upstairs I expect. Don't remember.

PHYLLY: Okay your side Mo?

MO: Hold it steady.

DANIELLE: Bet you didn't sleep much.

KATH: I heard her cry out but I didn't go.

PHYLLY: Kath – have you got the fly there?

KATH: What?

DANIELLE: Here.

PHYLLY: Throw it across!

> (*Keeping hold of her side, KATH throws the fly, like a sheet over a bed. PHYLLY catches it. The three women fasten it to the top of the tent.*)

DANIELLE: But I was okay?

KATH: Sorry?

DANIELLE: When Gran shouted out.

KATH: Yes. But she wasn't. If I'd gone to her…she might have…

DANIELLE: What?

KATH: Survived.

DANIELLE: When are you talking about?

KATH: Nothing.

PHYLLY: Peg it down and we're there.

> (*MO hammers in the pegs her side.*)

DANIELLE: Mum?

KATH: Just ghosts. Must be the mist.

MO: Catch!

> (*MO throws the hammer to PHYLLY who hammers in her pegs. The tent is up and has been achieved – miraculously – without argument and like clockwork.*)

PHYLLY: Not bad. Dave would be proud of us.

MO: He would, wouldn't he?

PHYLLY: Well, compared to the balls up we made of it last week, things are looking up. Danny, take a photo, we did it. I want it on record. We put up the tent. Outdoors. Up a hill.

MO: In the mist.

PHYLLY: By ourselves.

> (*The three women pose in front of the tent while DAN-IELLE takes the photo.*)

DANIELLE: And indeed there is a photo surviving showing three women wreathed in grey cobwebs of mist in front of a tent, on the summit of a hill, the light fading. What it doesn't show is how the tent got there, in what manner it was erected, with what degree of co-operation nor what happened next. That's left to memory, the most fickle storyteller of all.

(*The women are sat at the mouth of the tent having a last hot drink before bed. PHYLLY pours a tot of brandy into each of their enamel cups except DANIELLE's.*)

MO: These are very rustic.

PHYLLY: Well I'm not going to bring the bleeding Waterford am I?

MO: Not very…well…Brian, though are they?

PHYLLY: You mean they haven't got a logo.

KATH I'm just going out for a very short walk in order to take a very long pee.

MO: Was he the one in the photo who went up Everest with no trousers on?

PHYLLY: That was Mallory. And I don't think he was bare-arsed all the way.

MO: Why d'you think he did that?

PHYLLY: Come on. You're the one having it off for England, why d'you think?

MO: How does my having sex with a trainee geography teacher young enough to be my son make me an expert on why upper class Englishmen climbed mountains in hobnail boots and no knickers?

PHYLLY: They still do, for all we know. Love's young dream not going well then?

MO: Why d'you say that?

PHYLLY: Just a feeling.

MO: Hmmm.

DANIELLE: D'you think Mum's all right?

MO: Well she did say it was going to be a very long pee.

DANIELLE: About Gran I mean. She's being a bit weird.

PHYLLY: Probably guilt. She always preferred your Grandad.

DANIELLE: Didn't everyone?

PHYLLY: Mum…never got what she wanted. He did. I think.

DANIELLE: He can't have wanted her to be ill all the time.

(*KATH comes quietly back.*)

PHYLLY: When she'd have her spells of mania, they'd eat up the air, so it seemed as if there was nothing else existing. They took over everything. In fact she was only in hospital three times. It just felt like forever because we were kids.

KATH: Four. There was the time you first left home. He had so much to put up with you never knew about.

PHYLLY: That's not true. He was just a bloke, not a saint.

KATH: You've forgotten how it was. He was the one everyone loved. With his jokes and his big laugh.

PHYLLY: And his wandering hands and his lumpy trousers.

KATH: What?

PHYLLY: You heard me.

KATH: What is the matter with you?

PHYLLY: Nothing. Maybe I'm just fed up with this fantasy man you've invented.

KATH: I didn't invent my father.

PHYLLY: The truth is, our father touched up anything in a skirt that couldn't run away fast enough. The fact that you chose never to see it just shows how blinkered you are and always have been.

KATH: You are sick. You are so sick.

PHYLLY: How d'you explain how friends of ours only came round once?

KATH: It was her, the moods and the tears.

PHYLLY: Bollocks. It was Dada. He was a groper. A fumbler. A dirty old man.

KATH: I don't know why you're doing this. But I'll never forgive you for it.

PHYLLY: It's the truth. I'm sorry. But it is.

KATH: You're confusing him with someone else, someone you knew before. Dada was never like that.

PHYLLY: I'm sorry. But he was. She knew.

KATH: Mum? Oh I might have known this is where it came from. I can just hear her.

PHYLLY: There were complaints. It never got as far as the police. People felt sorry for her.

KATH: He was a gregarious man. People were drawn to him, to his company. He liked to laugh, he was open, affectionate. Everything she wasn't. Maybe if she'd just had a bit more love for him…

PHYLLY: You're saying it was her fault?

KATH: You know when I was fifteen she told me that sex was just a mess on the sheets.

PHYLLY: Maybe it was for them. It's not an excuse.

KATH: I don't believe you. I think you made all this up, to fit your warped picture of what men are to you.

MO: Kath don't.

KATH: What, defend him? You were damaged when you came to us. Don't blame him for that. Don't you ever blame my father for what other men have done to you.

PHYLLY: I don't. He was in a class all of his own. Why do you think I left?

(*There's a sound from DANIELLE.*)

Danny I'm sorry.

KATH: Her name's Danielle.

PHYLLY: I didn't mean for you to hear all this.

KATH: Stay away from her.

MO: You two. This has got to stop.

KATH: I mean it. Do you understand me? You can taint everything else with your filthy lies but I won't let you damage her. This is one thing you will never have.

DANIELLE: It was around this time I think I began to see cracking up as a seam running through the distaff side of my family. When will it be my turn? Is that what's going to happen next? I don't think I've ever stopped wondering that. (*Picks up an album.*) But I had a perfectly happy childhood. You've only to look back at the photographs to see that. Nothing but parties and picnics, Santas and seasides – not a straightjacket in sight.

Scene 4

Autumn 1978. Chronological order: Eight.

KATH's sitting room. Blackout, during which CRAIG enters the tent. DANIELLE sits at the mouth. MO and KATH enter carrying a birthday cake already cut into segments and bearing five lit candles. They're singing 'Happy Birthday Dear Danielle'.

KATH: Come on Danielle. Blow.

(*DANIELLE blows out the candles, lights up. KATH and MO clap. As DANIELLE, with the help of MO, shares out the cake, KATH takes a photo.*)

MO: Now that is my idea of camping. Carpet, radiators, tele.

KATH: She's too little to sleep outside in it yet. Maybe in the summer.

MO: Did she not want any friends round to play in the tent?

KATH: Just the one. And I said no. He'd be here all the time if I showed the slightest encouragement.

MO: Shame. I don't know how that poor woman manages.

KATH: How do any of us?

MO: But you decided to give her Derek's clothes after all?

(*KATH looks at her.*)

I recognised his coat on one of the older lads.

KATH: He's got no reason to show his face here now has he?

(*To DANIELLE.*) We'll save this last piece for Grandad.

DANIELLE: Can you turn the light out?

KATH: What on earth for?

DANIELLE: So I can see the stars.

KATH: Funny child.

(*KATH leaves the one piece of cake, turns out the light, and she and MO exit with the rest.*
DANIELLE licks her fingers, then she tidies round the crumbs at the edge of the last piece of cake.
CRAIG slithers to the edge of the tent.)

CRAIG: Aah, can I have some?

DANIELLE: It's for my Grandad.

CRAIG: He won't know.

DANIELLE: He will too. He's probably looking through the crack in the door now. Testing for draughts. With his eye, like that. He sees lots of things that way.

(*They hear a noise.*)

Quick, in the tent.

CRAIG: Is it burglars?

DANIELLE: Sssh. I knew his smell straight off. You don't forget that, however long they've been gone. And whatever Mum said, I'd known all along he wouldn't forget my birthday. This was what I'd wanted. The best present of all.

My dad home. I bet he'd bought me a Simple Simon and a Princess Leah too. He was looking in drawers, just like a burglar. Dad?

DEREK: Oh my God. Who is it?

DANIELLE: It's me, Danny.

DEREK: You nearly give me a heart attack. Where's your mum?

DANIELLE: In the kitchen with Mo.

DEREK: What's that doing in here?

DANIELLE: It's for my birthday.

DEREK: Right. Many happy returns.

DANIELLE: I knew you wouldn't forget. D'you want some cake?

DEREK: Er…

DANIELLE: Go on.

DEREK: All right. Thanks.

DANIELLE: What's that? Is it a book?

DEREK: (*Trying to hide his passport.*) Sort of.

DANIELLE: With pictures?

DEREK: Just the one. Of me.

DANIELLE: Is it for me?

DEREK: Er not this one. No.

DANIELLE: I can take a photo, look! (*Snaps him with the camera KATH left behind.*)

DEREK: No!

DANIELLE: (*Frightened.*) I'm sorry.

DEREK: It's just. No one must know I've been here. It'll be our secret. Yeah?

DANIELLE: If you like, you can sleep in my tent with me tonight.

DEREK: I can't stop sweetheart.

DANIELLE: Oh.

DEREK: But I did bring you a present. (*Searches his pockets and comes up with a disposable lighter.*)

DANIELLE: There's no paper.

DEREK: I know. I didn't want to set it alight by accident and cause a fire. You know how careful you have to be. So I kept it like this. Specially. For your campfire. See? You have to hold it down. That's it. Then you let go and it goes out. Neat eh? I got to go now.

DANIELLE: Badminton?

DEREK: Something like that. Bye sweetheart. Don't tell your mum I've been here, eh? It'll only upset her. I'll see you very soon. I promise.

DANIELLE: Cross your heart

DEREK: And hope to die.

DANIELLE: See you later alligator?

DEREK: Bye.

DANIELLE: No, in a while crocodile. Say it Daddy.

DEREK: Jesus Danielle, let go of me! Look, look I'm sorry but if she…okay, see you soon little baboon. Where oh where little bear. On the bus…

DANIELLE: (*Happy now.*) Hippypotymus!
   (*DEREK exits.*
   CRAIG emerges from the tent.)

CRAIG: Let's see. I wish I got one of these.
   (*KATH enters.*)

KATH: Danielle? Bath time. (*She switches on the light.*) And what do you think you're doing?
   (*CRAIG says nothing, just looks at DANIELLE.*)
   Did you eat that cake?

CRAIG: No.

KATH: I don't believe you. We were saving that for Danielle's grandfather.

DANIELLE: He didn't eat it.

KATH: Who did then? Was it you?

DANIELLE: No.

KATH: This is what happens. I won't have lying.

DANIELLE: I'm not. I promise.

CRAIG: It's not her fault.

KATH: So it just disappeared? Into thin air?

DANIELLE: We didn't eat it.

KATH: So it's going to come back again miraculously is it?

DANIELLE: It wasn't us. It wasn't.

KATH: Go to your room. And you. Go home.

DANIELLE: It's not fair! We didn't do anything wrong. But she wouldn't listen. I hated it when she was disappointed in me. Her disapproval went on for ever – sometimes right up until bedtime. But the taste of injustice, I've never lost it, like the metallic tang of a cut knee licked clean of blood.

The photo never came out of course. Not enough light. Just a flare that could have been anyone. And what use is that to me? On the bus hippypotymus. (*Shuts the photo album and puts it in a bag.*) Hers. Baggage. Even now a suitcase in the hall never fails to reduce me to a state of familiar anxiety. People leave and they come back. That's life. No cause for panic attacks.

Scene 5

Late summer 1988. Chronological order: Sixteen.

DANIELLE: On this particular day nearing the end of the long hot summer, the suitcases were a sign of arrival of someone with a lot of money and not much taste. Dad? (*DANIELLE runs into the room. MO is there and PHYLLY.*)
Oh. Someone set fire to the sports hut.

MO: Again? That place is fated. Was anyone hurt?

DANIELLE: No. Why 'again'?

MO: You were probably too small to remember. It was a cricket hut in those days. You want to go and get yourself a snack?

DANIELLE: No thanks. Hi Phylly.
(*PHYLLY turns. She has a black eye.*)
Oh my God. What happened?

MO: Phylly had an accident.

DANIELLE: How?

PHYLLY: I accidentally walked into Uncle Brian's fist.

MO: Here, ice'll help.

DANIELLE: Does it hurt?

PHYLLY: Ow! Not if I don't touch it.

MO: Let me.

PHYLLY: It still hurts.

MO: Bastard. What was the row about?

PHYLLY: This and that.

MO: Danielle, you got homework tonight?

DANIELLE: Yes, but…

MO: Better get on with it eh?

DANIELLE: After all this time they're worried about what I hear?! (*Sits down opens her books and plugs in her earpieces. She doesn't actually switch the Walkman on though.*)

MO: Are the cases a gesture or what?

PHYLLY: I don't know yet.

MO: So? What was it about?

PHYLLY: He found out how I used to earn my money.

MO: How?

PHYLLY: Somebody must have told him, I suppose.
(*Beat.*)

MO: You mean, one of your old clients?

PHYLLY: Probably.

MO: Have you not been waiting for that to happen?

PHYLLY: It's not something most men brag about.

MO: No.

PHYLLY: Funny. I'd always thought Brian'd led rather a sheltered life. I was amazed at his vocabulary of abuse.

MO: Shame he didn't stick to words. Has he done this before?

PHYLLY: No, of course not.
(*MO looks at her.*)
Nothing like.

MO: What d'you mean?

PHYLLY: Sometimes he'd just you know, hold onto my hand a bit hard. He's stronger than me. He'd always apologise afterwards. I think I made him nervous in public.

MO: You're excusing him?

PHYLLY: Maybe we're two of a kind. (*Suddenly exhausted.*)
I thought I was done with all this, Mo.
(*MO strokes her hair.*)
I worked, Jesus Christ how hard, to come through. I didn't want to leave here, but the dreams that wouldn't stop, the eye glinting through the keyhole that gradually took over the room, I had to. I don't want to have to go back to that place again. Do you know what I'm talking about?

MO: I'm not sure. Go on.

PHYLLY: You know he used to spy on us. He called it checking up.

MO: Your father?
(*PHYLLY nods.*)

Did he…ever…you know?

PHYLLY: Do it to me? No. He just let me know he could, any time he chose. He was in charge. I caught him once peering through a crack in the bathroom door. Kath was in there. I stayed out late that night and when I came back he put my fingers in the doorjamb and shut it. After that I was always accident prone. Tell me, was it you gave him my address in London?

MO: Sort of. I'm sorry. I didn't know not to. He came to see you?

PHYLLY: Oh yes. On my doorstep off the milk train. Didn't take him long to work it out. He was so angry his lips disappeared into a thin line pulled back over his teeth. Like an animal, growling. No daughter of mine. I thought he was going to kill me. As you see, he didn't. Bones break and bones mend. I came to his funeral to make sure he was dead. So I could come home again.

MO: Why didn't you tell us?

PHYLLY: How could I?

MO: But you got help from someone, somewhere along the line?

PHYLLY: I wouldn't be here otherwise. She was a small woman, called Mary. Neat white blouses with collars, and a cross on a chain round her throat. I used to look at that a lot. She sat very still and calm as if she didn't know she held the rest of my life in her hands. She held hope out to me if I would only dare to crawl back into those dark corners. And I did. I did. I thought I was safe now.
(*MO holds her as she cries.*)
What is it about me? Do I give out signals, shrill sounds only men like him can hear? Come on. Here I am, use me?
(*MO rocks PHYLLY. After a moment, PHYLLY suddenly sits up, looks over at DANIELLE ostensibly engrossed in her homework, brushes away her tears.*)
Hey enough of this.

MO: Phylly.

PHYLLY: I don't want to talk about it anymore.

MO: Okay.

PHYLLY: So, how was your day?

MO: As ever.

PHYLLY: Good. Good.

MO: Why have you come here now?

PHYLLY: I dunno.

MO: Have you two made it up?

PHYLLY: No.

MO: So?

PHYLLY: Nowhere else to go I suppose.

> (*Look from MO.*)
>
> Thought you might be, you know…swinging from the chandeliers?
>
> (*MO keeps on looking at her.*)
>
> They're murder to hang on to. Aha here she is.
>
> (*KATH enters. She looks surprised to see PHYLLY.*)

KATH: What're you doing here?

PHYLLY: Aren't you going to ask about my eye?

KATH: I assume somebody hit you.

PHYLLY: No surprise then?

MO: It was Brian. The bastard.

KATH: He always seemed such a kind, reasonable man to me.

PHYLLY: Meaning?

KATH: We all know you can be very provocative.

MO: Jesus Kath!

KATH: Are you going away?

PHYLLY: I'm afraid the climb's off.

KATH: Really.

PHYLLY: No Brian, no climb.

MO: We've got other sponsorship. We don't need him.

PHYLLY: We do. The air fares. If they're not paid for, we won't raise any money at all.

MO: We'll think of something.

PHYLLY: Without him we can't afford to go.

MO: It doesn't matter.

PHYLLY: Yes it does. Doesn't it, Kath? I mean, I let you down didn't I? Didn't I? That's what this is about, isn't it?

MO: (*Looking over at DANIELLE.*) Listen you two…

PHYLLY: Well? Have I got it wrong. I thought this was all my fault. No?

KATH: I don't know what you're talking about.

PHYLLY: So, is this quits now? Or what? (*She gestures to her face.*)

KATH: You make the life you get, Phylly.
(*Beat.*)

MO: Come on. You can stay at my place.

KATH: I thought we were spending the evening together.

MO: Not tonight Kath.

KATH: But we had plans.
(*MO picks up the suitcases and exits with PHYLLY.*)
Danielle? Danielle?
(*DANIELLE remains engrossed in her books. KATH believes she can't hear her.*)
(*Whispering.*) I love you so much. Help me.
(*KATH sits in a chair and closes her eyes. DANIELLE looks up. She has of course heard every word.*)

DANIELLE: Even now those words feel like insects crawling along my spine. Sometimes I'd wake to find her stroking my face. His face as she called it. I sleep with the light on.

Scene 6

Summer 1977. Chronological order: Two.

DANIELLE: Sentry duty by the front door. Myself and my Mum on the lookout for The Man in White. He left this morning with the bag containing the white clothes, the nobbly heavy jumper with dented roads down it for rolling marbles, the soft creamy white trousers with the red stain on the pocket and no telling off for spilling your juice. This is for cricket. At four I am learning sports sartorially. My mum is anxious, her heels pecking between kitchen and front step, her mouth fidgeting off her lipstick. Maybe the mark on the trousers is lipstick but why would she kiss his pocket smearing towards the zip on Wednesday nights and then the laundry to complain of on Thursday? She is going out with 'the girls'. With Mo and Phylly. And my Dad is taking care of me.
(*DEREK enters in a rush, throwing down his bag. He's wearing suit trousers and a shirt. He and KATH go into the kitchen, DANIELLE remains on the stairs.*)

DEREK: Sorry I'm late.

KATH: Where the hell have you been? Derek?

DEREK: What d'you mean? It's Wednesday.

KATH: I know what day it is. Thank God you're all right.
I was about to ring the police.

(*PHYLLY enters. She too is wearing bright lipstick.*)

PHYLLY: Where were you going in such an almighty hurry?
Hi Kath. Jumping red lights all down King Street.

DEREK: I didn't see you.

PHYLLY: I should think everything was a bit of a blur at that
speed.

KATH: You could have at least phoned. I was so worried.

DEREK: I'm not that late am I?

PHYLLY: Did you hear about the fire on the radio?

KATH: No, Mo phoned. She said no one was seriously hurt
but when you didn't come home.

DEREK: What did they say on the radio?

PHYLLY: That there's not much of the cricket club left. It
went up like a tinderbox.

DEREK: Yes, it was dreadful. I got caught up so by the time I
arrived the road was blocked.

KATH: What did you do?

DEREK: You know. What I could really. Helped out. Gave
some old bloke a lift home. It was pretty shocking.

PHYLLY: Must have been.

DEREK: One minute it's there, the next everything's up in
flames. Tell you the truth I'm still a bit shaken.

KATH: Poor love. I'll put your tea on.

DEREK: Thanks sweetheart. Sorry I worried you. I just didn't
notice the time, you know, rushing to and fro.

KATH: As long as you're safe.

(*KATH exits.*
PHYLLY gives him a long hard look.)

PHYLLY: Don't look so pleased with yourself.

DEREK: Thanks pal.

PHYLLY: Next time you see me flashing my lights, consider it
might be for a reason, not just a bloody car chase.

DEREK: I'll bear that in mind.

PHYLLY: If I hadn't had the local radio on, you wouldn't
have had a clue would you? Then what would you have
done?

DEREK: I'd have thought of something.

PHYLLY: I hope she was worth it.

DEREK: It's not my fault. She was always there at cricket practice.

PHYLLY: Change your sport then.

DEREK: Might just do that. Fancy a spot of badminton? I might take it up again. What d'you say?

PHYLLY: No thanks. Been there, done that.

DEREK: Shame. Thanks anyway. I owe you one. (*Gives her a kiss on the cheek which turns into a hug.*) Remember the baths. In the changing room after school swimming. Oh yes. You do remember.

PHYLLY: I do yeah. (*Beat.*) But then my motto wasn't fuck em and forget em was it?

DEREK: Oh come on. You were willing. You've always been willing.

PHYLLY: Get off.

DEREK: (*Laughing.*) No sweat. We were just kids.

PHYLLY: We were certainly that.

DEREK: We had to move on at some point.

PHYLLY: True. Is this conversation going anywhere?

DEREK: We were two of a kind. Still are.

PHYLLY: But I always knew I was damaged goods.

DEREK: Sorry.

(*PHYLLY shrugs.*)

I was a little shit wasn't I?

PHYLLY: And now you're a big one. Evolution at work.

DEREK: How come you never warned her off me?

PHYLLY: I did. She thought I was jealous.

DEREK: And were you?

PHYLLY: Of her?

DEREK: You always had a string of boyfriends.

PHYLLY: Anyway, she needed to leave home.

DEREK: Yeah well we're still waiting for that to happen. This isn't all my fault you know.

PHYLLY: Oh please.

DEREK: I can't compete with him. Nobody could. I did try.

(*PHYLLY pats his arm. She understands what he's been up against. He holds on to her.*)

Maybe if it'd been you…

(*PHYLLY tries to move away.*)

Thanks for not blowing the whistle on me.

PHYLLY: It's not for your sake.

DEREK: I should have stayed with you.

PHYLLY: Don't. And don't count on my silence for ever.
Contrary to public opinion I am not made of fucking stone.

DEREK: Is that a threat Phyllida?

PHYLLY: Whatever.

DEREK: You know something. If Kath ever caught me with
you, you'd be the one she'd never forgive.
(*KATH enters.*)

KATH: Give us your whites and I'll put a load on. They must
be all filth and smokey.

DEREK: No, you get off out and have yourselves a good time.
I'll see to it. Danielle can help me.

DANIELLE: And I did. Willingly. Together we washed away
a scent that was not there, tumbled and lathered white cot-
ton that was already, as my grandmother would say, pure
as the driven snow and laughed. He gave me pieces of his
supper on a small plate and for afters we ate creamed rice
straight out of the tin with teaspoons, sweet as memory.
(*Pours and swigs a glass of wine in an attempt to erase the pain.*)

Scene 7

Autumn 1988. Chronological order: Seventeen.

*MO is in her garden on the cordless phone, surrounded by
rucksacks, ground sheets and mountain paraphernalia.*

MO: (*On phone.*)Well maybe you should take her at face value,
believe what she says.
(*PHYLLY enters wearing MO's track pants and carrying
a pillow.*)

PHYLLY: What d'you think? My pink ones aren't practical so
I borrowed yours instead. You don't mind do you?
(*Before MO can say anything PHYLLY carries on, as does
the caller. MO's trapped.*)
You're out of juice by the way.

MO: Fine. (*On phone.*) Sorry, no. Does it feel like emotional
blackmail to you though?

PHYLLY: Of course I'm longer in the leg than you but they'll stretch. (*Drops the pillow on the ground and starts to unpack a rucksack.*)

MO: I've just packed that! (*On phone.*) Sorry, what?

(*DANIELLE enters.*)

PHYLLY: (*Surprised.*) Oh hello. Are you…?

DANIELLE: She'd kill me if she knew I was here.

PHYLLY: Big risk.

DANIELLE: Heard you were going to do the climb after all.

PHYLLY: Well 'a' climb. Having got this far…

DANIELLE: Right. And if people are prepared to sponsor you.

PHYLLY: Exactly. It doesn't have to be exotic and foreign.

DANIELLE: I thought you said Wales.

PHYLLY: All right, it doesn't have to be exotic.

MO: (*On phone.*) If you feel you ought to be there, then go, that's fine. I really don't mind.

PHYLLY: As long as it involves effort and challenge. Mo agrees. Don't you?

MO: (*On phone.*) Really, I promise you.

PHYLLY: She does. A mountain's a mountain. You come to wave us off?

DANIELLE: Could you fit just one more thing in?

PHYLLY: Like where?

DANIELLE: Please? It's only little.

PHYLLY: What is it then?

(*DANIELLE gets out Gran's urn from her bag.*)

Mum! I did wonder.

DANIELLE: I wanted to stop you two fighting about them.

PHYLLY: We've fought all our lives.

DANIELLE: Does that make it a good thing?

(*PHYLLY smiles and takes the urn.*)

DANIELLE: I was fond of her.

PHYLLY: Me too.

MO: (*On phone.*) Truthfully, I wouldn't mind.

DANIELLE: Phylly, can I ask you something, hypothetically?

PHYLLY: Sure.

DANIELLE: You said there were fires round here once.

PHYLLY: A fire, yes.

DANIELLE: If you knew, or thought you knew, who'd set them, it, would you have done anything about it? You know, told anyone? I mean, it's sort of betrayal isn't it?

PHYLLY: Sometimes it's necessary. Nicola needs the kind of help you can't give, Danny.

DANIELLE: How did you know?

PHYLLY: You haven't seen the paper this week. There was a big picture, TEENAGE ARSONIST ARRESTED.

DANIELLE: Was she wearing long sleeves?

PHYLLY: I don't remember.

DANIELLE: She doesn't like to show her arms. She'll not forgive me.

PHYLLY: She may need to.

MO: Yeah, you too. Bye…. Bye. (*Hanging up.*) Honestly.

PHYLLY: What?

MO: I sometimes wonder…you know…is it worth it?

PHYLLY: He'll be alright.

MO: He's so wound up about this party his father's giving and whether he should go or if it would be disloyal to his mother…or if I should go. I mean, God forbid. I'm not even family. Hello Danielle.

DANIELLE: Dave let me in. Sorry.

MO: Don't be silly. I'm pleased to see you. Really.
(*As long as I'm not with Mum, thinks DANIELLE.*)
Everything, you know, all right?
(*DANIELLE nods.*)
I left a message. Several actually.

PHYLLY: Saying what?

MO: Never mind.

PHYLLY: 'Hi Kath, the black eye's fading, you treacherous bitch. Come on round.'?

MO: You don't know it was her told Brian.

PHYLLY: No, it was probably the fucking tooth fairy. And what happened to 'we'? As in 'We don't know it was her'?

MO: I don't like gangs.
(*PHYLLY looks at her.*)

PHYLLY: So, are we packing or what?

MO: Before we go I've got to take the cat to the vet.

PHYLLY: It's perfectly all right.

MO: It was sick. In the bath.

PHYLLY: Easier to clean up. The cat shows consideration, you take it to the vet, where's the justice in that?

MO: Have you ever taken care of anything?

PHYLLY: It was a joke. The cat's not offended for Christ's sake. Look, Danielle's here to help, so are we driving to Wales this afternoon or what?

MO: I couldn't even feed him this morning cos there was no milk.

PHYLLY: How is that my fault?

MO: Because you drank it. Just like you've drunk everything else you've set your eyes since you moved in.

PHYLLY: You said to make myself at home. If you didn't mean it you shouldn't have…

MO: Nobody else here behaves like you – not even the teenagers. You use everything, take everything as if it's all yours by right. It's like having some…some feral creature in the house. And if you're not going back to Brian, I think it's about time you found a place of your own.

PHYLLY: What have I done wrong?

MO: I don't want to look after you any more. That's all. Quite simple really. I am fed up with always taking care of everyone, of being taken for granted. I mean, for Christ's sake I can't even have a straightforward extra marital affair without him expecting me to sort his emotional socks into pairs. Well, enough.

(*DAVE enters with the cat basket.*)

What do you want?

DAVE: (*Waving the cat basket.*) The cat?

MO: No idea.

(*DAVE exits stoically.*)

And what is more we didn't need to do all those press ups.

PHYLLY: Sorry?

MO: You don't need great broad shoulders to walk up a mountain. You need stamina and believe me, dealing with you and Kath for thirty years has given me plenty of that. So get your own trousers on, put my pillow back indoors where it belongs, and don't put anything that isn't yours inside that rucksack. Understood?

PHYLLY: Perfectly.

MO: I'm sorry, but I think it's time I spoke my mind.

PHYLLY: Absolutely.

(*Blast of 'Staying Alive' from off.*)

MO: Dave! Dave! For God's sake!

PHYLLY: I take it things aren't going so swimmingly with whatisname then?

MO: Oh he's affectionate, sings like an angel, can keep it up for hours...

PHYLLY: But?

MO: I didn't say there was a but.

PHYLLY: I thought you were speaking your mind today.

(*Phone rings. DAVE comes out.*)

MO: I am. What are you doing?

DAVE: Finding you some music for your Walkman. Cat's gone under the bed and won't come out. Shall I?

MO: No! It's probably about the rehearsal next week. Carry on without me.

DAVE: I'd rather not.

MO: (*On phone.*) Hello? Nothing... I'm absolutely bloody fine!

DAVE: Remember this Danielle? Bet you can't do it.

DANIELLE: I wouldn't want to.

DAVE: Chicken.

(*He starts to do the 'Staying Alive' dance. DANIELLE joins in.*)

MO: (*On phone.*) No, I didn't mean that. (*Hand over phone.*) What are you doing?

DAVE: Staying Alive. Dancing. Come on Phylly, join in.

(*PHYLLY does so.*)

MO: Well don't, you look ridiculous. (*On phone.*) No not you.

DANIELLE: Oh my God, how sad are we?

MO: (*On phone.*) I can't, not now. I'll speak to you later. (*Rings off.*) Stop it, Dave please!

DAVE: Sorry.

MO: Oh for Christ's sake. How can you just stand there, jigging about. You know what's going on. How can you just jig about while I'm...while we're...

DAVE: I don't know what else to do. What d'you want me to do?

MO: Just do...something!

(*Phone rings again.*)

(*On phone.*) What? No, I can't.

(*DAVE hesitates then grabs the phone.*)

DAVE: Didn't you hear her? She can't... Because she says so and Mo knows what she wants. And whatever that is, it'll be for the best. If you don't know that about her, you know nothing. In fact I bet you don't even know what her luxury on a desert island'd be. (*Beat.*) Exactly. (*Snaps the aerial off and throws the phone over his shoulder.*) I think you'll find it's a hot water bottle. Now if you'll excuse me, I've to take our cat to the vet. (*Exits.*)

(*MO watches him go, open mouthed. She smiles.*)

PHYLLY: Are we going then?

MO: I think it's time, don't you?

PHYLLY: And beyond. We're one down, sure you don't want to join us Danny?

DANIELLE: I thought I might you know, ring and see when visiting hours are. (*Exits.*)

MO: I think our phone's out of order.

(*Staying Alive' is turned off.*)

Can you believe all this?

PHYLLY: It's going to be a hell of a squash.

MO: In your car? Come on.

(*BRIAN enters, followed by DANIELLE.*)

DANIELLE: I'm sorry but...

BRIAN: (*Entering.*) I only want to see her, that's all.

MO: We're just off.

PHYLLY: Yeah, we're actually going. Sorry to disappoint you.

BRIAN: Sometimes I feel nothing could ever disappoint me again. So where does this event take place?

PHYLLY: Did you come to wish us luck?

BRIAN: I came to talk to you.

PHYLLY: So here I am.

BRIAN: Preferably out of earshot of the coven.

MO: Excuse me, this is my garden.

BRIAN: And my wife.

PHYLLY: It's all right. Really. I'll shout if I need you.

MO: We'll just be inside.

(*MO and DANIELLE reluctantly leave. DANIELLE creeps back to watch from the side.*)

BRIAN: Thank you. You look…brilliant

PHYLLY: I'm good at make-up.

BRIAN: I can't believe it happened. I'm so sorry.

PHYLLY: We've been over all this.

BRIAN: I'm not like this. I'm a nice bloke. It was just the shock.

PHYLLY: I'm still the same person.

BRIAN: I know. I just wish you hadn't lied to me.

PHYLLY: Would you have married me if I hadn't? Honestly?

BRIAN: I'm trying to wipe it out of my mind. I'm doing my best.

PHYLLY: You could try harder.

BRIAN: I feel used.

PHYLLY: How exactly? Weren't we both getting what we wanted? Marriage is a deal, isn't it?

BRIAN: I gave you everything.

PHYLLY: Thank you.

BRIAN: All I asked in return was love.

PHYLLY: I did my best.

BRIAN: I think you were overpaid.

(*PHYLLY goes to slap him; he catches her hand, holds it tenderly.*)

Come on, we're two of a kind. You need me. I know you. I know what works for you. It's all right. Come back now and we'll start again.

PHYLLY: How?

BRIAN: We know where we are now. Nothing to hide. I've said I'm sorry.

PHYLLY: Yeah. I heard you.

BRIAN: And I forgive you.

PHYLLY: Oh good. Now I'll be able to sleep again.

BRIAN: I'm serious Phyllida, I'm prepared to take you back. This can be all in the past. No one else need know. It'll be our secret.

PHYLLY: And if I don't want to come?

BRIAN: But you must! I need you. (*Beat.*) Then the deal's off. I want the keys back. The house, the car, the lot.

PHYLLY: We'll sort this out later. We're driving to Wales now.

BRIAN: What in?

PHYLLY: Oh don't be petty.

BRIAN: I'd like the keys to my car please.

PHYLLY: Brian!

> (*PHYLLY's hand goes automatically to her pocket for the keys. BRIAN sees and he holds out his hand.*)

BRIAN: Now, please. (*Takes PHYLLY's hand containing the keys.*) There's a good girl. Come on. Let's forget all this …silliness. You don't want to go fooling around climbing mountains at your age. What's the point? You go up, you come down, what's changed? Life goes on, just like it always has. (*All the time he is squeezing PHYLLY's hand.*)

> (*KATH enters.*)

KATH: What's going on?

BRIAN: Stay out of this.

PHYLLY: Don't please.

> (*BRIAN is squeezing her fingers hard.*)

KATH: Leave her alone, Brian.

BRIAN: Give me the keys. Time to stop taking what isn't yours. Eh Kath?

KATH: I don't know what you mean.

BRIAN: You started this. You know what she is. You told me.

> (*BRIAN increases his pressure on PHYLLY's hand. She gasps.*)

KATH: She's my sister, that's who she is.

> (*KATH hits BRIAN on the chin; he falls in shock more than pain.*
> *MO and DANIELLE run on.*)

MO: Oh my god!

> (*KATH is clutching her hand.*)

BRIAN: You hit me!

KATH: Shit, shit, shit.

MO: Phylly are you okay?

BRIAN: She hit me!

MO: Who did?

BRIAN: That's assault.

PHYLLY: You should know.

BRIAN: I'll sue you for this.

MO: I'm going to call Dave.

BRIAN: (*Going.*) Call who you like. (*To PHYLLY.*) You're done, finished.

MO: That's it. Out, now!

KATH: Will you stop talking to the arsehole and fucking somebody do something about my fucking hand!

DANIELLE: Mum!

(*MO sees BRIAN off.*)

PHYLLY: Where does it hurt?

KATH: Fucking everywhere.

DANIELLE: Mum.

KATH: What, for fuck's sake?

DANIELLE: Nothing.

PHYLLY: Wiggle your fingers. Good.

KATH: I am never doing that again.(*Astonished.*) It really hurts hitting people!

(*PHYLLY is holding KATH's sore hand. KATH looks up into her face. MO holds her breath.*)

PHYLLY: What're you doing here?

KATH: The phone wasn't working.

PHYLLY: Couldn't bear to be left out, could you?

KATH: No. I just dropped by. To wish you luck.

MO: Wearing shorts and big boots?

KATH: Ah. (*She has to smile.*) What do you reckon?

PHYLLY: There'll be nobody there except sheep to see us. And anyway, do we care?

(*Laughing, they stand, with their arms round each others necks as if in a photo, looking into the camera. DANIELLE looks round her at all the boxes.*)

DANIELLE: I will miss...the intimacy. But it's not the answer, maybe no one person ever is and – truth told – I don't think I liked him very much. If only I'd acknowledged that at the beginning. But you have to believe everything's going to work out fine in the end. Don't you? Otherwise you'd never start anything.

It seems to me we remain fixed on the same track for so many years and then one day we change direction, our vision widens, there is depth of field. Why at that moment, that place, that time? Not only loss, surely? Was someone signalling from a hilltop far off? A flash of light we were not aware of seeing? A piece of mirror maybe? In the sliver of glass held up to my childhood I see in the beginning, with no hint of the false memory of photographs, a kitchen, at night, and three women. Three women smelling of babies, tomatoes and cheap red wine. A sort of triangular recipe for migraine I suppose.

Scene 8

Spring 1977. Chronological order: One.

KATH's house. PHYLLY and MO pose as DANIELLE, aged four, takes a photo.

MO: Point it up. Can you see our faces?

KATH: She'll ruin it.

PHYLLY: Doesn't matter. We'll have a lasting memento of our knees.

MO: Well done love.

KATH: Now, off to bed. I'll be up in a minute.

(*DANIELLE sits on the stairs.*)

MO: What did Derek give you?

KATH: This, isn't it sweet. (*Shows off a chain round her neck.*) It's got a little fish on it, see. To remind me of how we first met.

PHYLLY: The chippy?

KATH: The swimming baths. But the best one, the absolute bestest one in the world is outside. Look.

MO: A greenhouse?

KATH: Isn't it wonderful? Dada knew I'd always wanted one and a man at his allotments died so it was going cheap. Derek worked all yesterday transferring it.

MO: Good for him.

PHYLLY: Where's your back yard gone?

KATH: There's plenty of room.

PHYLLY: And Danny plays where?

KATH: She'll help me. We can grow tomatoes and sweet peas just like Dada does. We'll share packets of seeds and give each other cuttings. I can't wait to get started.

MO: You've got it all worked out.

KATH: I know it's only little but it's a beginning. I can dream.

PHYLLY: Come on, cut the cake. Okay. Three wishes each.

KATH: Me first. I'd have my own market garden. Derek and I would have four children and and...

PHYLLY: Hurry up or I'll have your last one.

KATH: You won't. I'll save it for now.

MO: I'd have…

PHYLLY: Travel the world, win the pools and be beautiful.

MO: No children?

PHYLLY: If I'm rich I can have what I want, that includes kids and a big house and no one telling me what to do or what time I'm supposed to be anywhere.

KATH: You got fired again didn't you?

PHYLLY: I quit.

KATH: Oh Phylly.

PHYLLY: Don't want to talk about it. I'll get something somewhere else. Don't look so worried. I'll survive. Don't I always? Worst comes to the worst and the Christmas post round is filled with poxy students I'll just marry a rich man instead.

KATH: Better get a move on, they get snapped up early.

PHYLLY: Then I'll just have to have someone else's cast off.

MO: Make sure he's kind. And funny. With muscular buttocks. And lots of hair.

PHYLLY: On his bum?

KATH: On his head.

MO: And a taut stomach.

PHYLLY: With one of those little lines of hair going down to…

MO: Definitely.

KATH: Oh yes. Derek's got one of those.

PHYLLY: So, what're your three Mo?

MO: Well I've got everything I could wish for really. Dave's all of those things, except rich. And I've got my boys and a job that has school holidays and two of the best friends in the world.

PHYLLY: Don't get sentimental on us. You must want something, you're too young to be smug.

MO: All right then. I want everyone to be happy and everything to stay just as it is, now.

PHYLLY: And world peace?

KATH: Don't be so mean.

PHYLLY: Sorry. Can't help it.

MO: To now.

KATH: To us.

(*There is an almighty crash offstage of breaking glass.*)

PHYLLY: Oops.

MO: Oh no. Not your present!

(*KATH rushes off stage. There is a shriek of rage.*)

KATH: (*Off.*) I'll kill you. You little shits.

PHYLLY: Well that's world peace put on hold.

(*Another scream of rage off.*)

MO: Do you think we ought to…?

PHYLLY: Not with all that broken glass around.

MO: Kath?

(*KATH enters slowly carrying an old football.*)

I'm so sorry.

KATH: They've ruined everything.

PHYLLY: I'm sure it wasn't on purpose. They're just kids.

KATH: They're out of control. People like Dan McGellan and his family spoil everything for everyone else.

MO: You've still got a wish left.

PHYLLY: This ought to be good.

KATH: I wish…

(*DANIELLE puts the football back in the understairs cupboard. Closes a suitcase. Looks around. Dawn is breaking outside her room.*)

DANIELLE: Maybe that's it. There aren't any resolutions – though I do wish there were. Instead just plateaux every now and then where you can take stock, look around you, before setting off again. It's a lonely prospect but then I look back and there, now I see clearly, the light behind her, Phylly. Aglow, surviving. Damaged, invincible Phylly. And Mo, waving. I see, in effect, my guardian angels. And Mum, miraculously straighter between the two of them. And I always thought you shrank with age. Some stories that are handed down are true. And some are just handed down. Maybe moving on is working out which is which. Or trying to anyway. When I consider Phylly and all those other children whose faces look at you from newspapers every day, it strikes me that merely surviving, with even a hint of grace and joy, is something of a miracle.

(Leaving the rest of the baggage behind her, DANIELLE picks up her camera and a small backpack. She opens the door, the light floods in as she passes through, illuminating the three women standing together.)

End.

Rise Up
9781783199938

Keep Smiling Through
9781849430142

Once We Were Mothers
9781840024999

Stamping, Shouting and Singing Home
9781840027037

The Day The Waters Came
9781849431019